Peaceful Parenting

10 Essential Principles

by

Marianne Clyde

ISBN: 1482687976
ISBN-13: 9781482687972
Library of Congress Control Number: 2013905251
CreateSpace Independent Publishing Platform
North Charleston, South Carolina

MommyZEN
Warrenton, Virginia, USA

DEDICATED TO

Jedidiah, Madison, Ryan, Devon, Roba, Sean,
Thomas, Samantha, Mae, and Cayson,
my awesome grandchildren.
You are the generation that will soon rule the world.

Contents

Acknowledgements

Susan McCorkindale, there is no way that I could have done this without you. Thanks for your honesty, your encouragement, and your skill as a best-selling writer and editor. And of course, thanks to the rest of my team: Shari Goodwin, a phenomenal, inspiring coach, and Yvonne Herbst, who so patiently and expertly edited blogs and articles that ultimately became a part of this book and who also advised me on social media.

My kids and step-kids and your spouses who created material for the book just by being who you are, I thank you for allowing me to witness your evolution into amazing, creative, mindful, and authentic adults and parents.

And to my husband, Bob, whose encouragement and belief in me keeps me moving forward, thank you.

To the creator of the universe who lives in me and waits patiently for me to allow him to be manifested in my life, you are in fact "Christ in me, the hope of glory," and you have a message of encouragement and hope that you have given me to share. I am in awe of your love.

FOREWORD

First of all, I love the title that gives the outcome of the practice: *Peaceful* Parenting. We hear a lot of advice that generally ends in guilt! Guilt is a long distance from peace.

I have traveled with Marianne in some of the most troubled countries in our world today. There were times we should have been fearful and allowed the fear to control us, but she exercised the principles as noted in this book, and all in her presence were at peace.

However, Marianne is no "Pollyanna." She is aware of reality. She has lived in chaos and uncertainty. Through these experiences, she has forged these principles with the anvil of pain and success.

This book is one I wish I would have had many years ago. I well remember throwing a parenting book across the room and saying rather forcefully, "Give me an author who has lived in the chaos of raising four children." Well, Marianne has raised more than four children and has experienced that of putting families and children together.

The added texture to this book is not only that of Marianne's personal experience but that of her education and the many years in the counseling room as a family therapist. But there is still one more addition that makes a difference: the spiritual dimension. These are the depths this book probes to bring out the lasting peace that comes from God.

I commend this book to you to carry in your pocket for a quick refresher, on your iPad or iPhone, or in your head. It will be transformative in all your life.

JoAnne Lyon, *General Superintendent of the Wesleyan Church, founder of World Hope International, and author of* The Ultimate Blessing.

INTRODUCTION

My fifteen-year-old daughter came home after a week at church camp and greeted me with, "I need to go live with Dad"—or some such nonsense. I don't really remember her exact words because I felt like I had been knocked over by a two-by-four. I felt kind of dizzy and sick to my stomach. My thoughts began to race: *Oh my God. She hates me. I'm a terrible mother. There's no way I can let her do that!*

To my divorced and remarried mind, this was a huge blow to my ego, my parenting and my plan for my life—and a potential blow to my perceived reputation. (Notice the many uses of "my.") So after I shook the stars out of my head from that unexpected left hook—which honestly took several days—we talked and made plans for her dad to pick her up and take her to live with him in another state.

Watching them drive away, I could feel a part of my heart rip out of my chest, and I swallowed back the vomit that I felt rising up my throat. Then, I took a deep breath and turned around to go back inside to my ten-year-old son, who was probably wondering why he couldn't go too.

I healed my devastation by turning my thoughts to what was best for her. I couldn't base my decision on what I wanted and what worked for me; I had to consider her needs as a young teenage girl trying to find her way. And as any parent knows, a girl needs her dad sometimes. The truth is, as much as I wanted to be her everything, I couldn't be. As much as her stepdad loved her, he wasn't her dad. And like it or not, she had an opinion that I needed to listen to and a voice that I needed to respect.

I knew I couldn't let other people's opinions influence my decision. I had to realize that, even though things hurt sometimes, I needed to look at the bigger picture. At that time, I had been a therapist for about four years and had taught parenting classes. Ironically, my daughter expressed concern that it might look bad for me as a "parenting expert" to have my own child leave home. It's funny how—after I got over the initial trauma of her announcement—I could tell her the importance of not letting other people's opinions guide these kinds of decisions. Like Hannah from days gone by, I needed to let go.

Hannah, if you don't know, was a mom who knew the heartache and devastation of allowing the opinions of others to determine her self-worth. But she wasn't always a mom. Longing for a dream that seemed so elusive for her, she prayed for a child. She wanted a child so desperately that she promised God if he would just bless her with a son, she would dedicate him to God for all the days of his life.

And God heard her. In due time, Hannah conceived and gave birth to a son. Unlike many of us who beg God for something and make big promises in our misery, Hannah did not go back on her promise. When she weaned her son, she took him to the temple to serve God all his days.

That takes faith. It takes trust in God. It means letting go of the micromanaging and obsessing.

It implies that she trusted God to work his plan in her son's life. It means that she had such a connection to—and faith in—her creator that she felt at peace enough to let go. This book is about letting go. It's about trusting. It's about being at peace with yourself and with God and helping your child to find that centered place. It's really very simple; it's just not easy.

6Because the Lord had closed Hannah's womb, her rival kept provoking her in order to irritate her. 7 This went on year after year. Whenever Hannah went up to the house of the Lord, her rival provoked her till she wept and would not eat. 8 Her husband Elkanah would say to her, "Hannah, why are you weeping? Why don't you eat? Why are you downhearted? Don't I mean more to you than ten sons?"

9 Once when they had finished eating and drinking in Shiloh, Hannah stood up. Now Eli the priest was sitting on his chair by the doorpost of the Lord's house. 10 In her deep anguish Hannah prayed to the Lord, weeping bitterly. 11 And she made a vow, saying, "Lord Almighty, if you will only look on your servant's misery and remember me, and not forget your servant but give her a son, then I will give him to the Lord for all the days of his life, [1 Samuel 1:6-11]

You can read Hannah's story in the Bible: 1 Samuel 1.

Can you imagine the backlash when Hannah took her son to the temple to live? "Oh my God, Hannah, what are you thinking? You prayed and prayed for that kid! Now you are going to just let him go?" But she knew what she needed to do, and she did it. She didn't allow the opinions of others to sway her.

Being an effective and loving parent has very little to do with what others think about you. It is not about controlling your child but controlling yourself: your thoughts, your words, your actions. It is about an awareness of how your words and actions in the present moment can affect your kids for the rest of their lives. Yes, sometimes being a parent hurts. It's not about covering up those hurts, but it's about sharing your feelings lovingly, calmly, and directly with your children so they can learn to do the same. It's not about stuffing negative feelings; it's about recognizing them, naming them, and dealing with them so your kids can too.

I began to find my voice. I started to trust my instincts more and more. The opinions of others began to fade to a dull irritation in the back of my mind. I had started my journey to live on my own terms. Not necessarily pain-free, but just plain free.

I retired from being perfect when I got my divorce. Perfection caused too much pressure: always trying to be what I thought everyone else thought I should be. (Wow—that line reads as a bit of a tongue twister.) Well then, I guess it pretty well describes my thinking back then—a little twisted. I would assume or guess what people expected from me and then try to do what I thought they thought I should do.

It could all have been resolved by straight communication: a bit of understanding about who I really am; a sense of security in trusting my own thoughts, judgments, and opinions—if I only knew what they were. But I was somehow convinced that everyone knew better than I. I felt pretty anxious back then. Yeah, no kidding: stomach issues, migraines. But you would never know because I became pretty good at spinning the plates. I danced to the music I thought I needed to dance to whether I liked the tune or not. Finally, I just got tired. I realized that I felt lonely, and that, try as I might, my communications were not being heard. I could see that my life wasn't going to change by itself. So I changed it.

I finally made a decision, and the migraines stopped. But the anxiety did not. I still hadn't learned how not to worry about what other people thought—especially when I had old friends showing up at my front door wanting to straighten me out or calling me on the phone telling me I was going to go to hell or die—really...no kidding. You would have felt anxious too.

So, now I even questioned my faith. Jeez, life can be so complicated sometimes.

Hannah struggled with these same thoughts and fears. She wanted so badly to be a mother. Her husband had another wife—a wife who kept producing children. And oh, how she gloated! The message rang clear: "Gee, Hannah, what's wrong with you?" The other wife played on the cultural shame that Hannah felt. Motherhood was her purpose, and she could not make it happen. She felt defective... incompetent...inferior.

Hannah's husband loved her; he even loved her more than his other wife. But that did not ease Hannah's heartache. Nothing could.

Nothing, that is, until she made a decision; until she got focused; until she put words to her desire and connected desperately to her creator as if her life and future depended on it. She connected to the true source of life and power and detached from all the noise and emotion of her culture, her immediate surroundings, and her shame. She realized that none of that really had any power. Her true power lay in her connection to her source, and from that rose the promise of fulfillment and life.

Like Hannah, I began to ask myself questions. What do I really believe—and why? Do my beliefs make sense to me, or am I parroting some Bible study teacher or pastor or my mother or some complete stranger who, for some reason, I trust more than my own mind? Like Hannah, I needed to clarify what I wanted, connect to my creator, and detach from the fears of what other people said or believed. My journey contained ups and downs that carried with them lessons, successes, and failures along the way. But from that journey, I learned the principle that Hannah learned and lived: the principle that gave her peace and fulfillment in ways beyond her wildest dreams.

I am sure there are days, probably many, when my little ones (the youngest of whom is now thirty) wish I had been a calm, focused, and more secure parent. I am sure they wish I had learned this principle a long time ago. But, you know, it is what it is. I can't change where I have been. I can only change where I am going.

The seed had been planted for this journey long ago: a seed found in such an unlikely place as an outlet store when my daughter was just four. It's been a long, hard, fun, crazy, and interesting trip from insecure wife and mother to MommyZen, but I want to share what I have learned along the way with you.

What on earth is MommyZen, and how does it relate to you? Well, the way I see it, it's a mind-set—a lifestyle. It's not a series of parenting techniques; although, I will share a bag of tricks with you. It's not a religion, even though I am a Christian. It's a state of being. I use a very broad definition of Zen to include a peaceful, confident, integrated, and mindful existence as it relates to all things—but particularly parenting. It's a concept that all faiths can easily embrace, and it encourages that. It creates a kind of energy: an atmosphere that encourages love and growth and peace even in the midst of chaos. It's a survival guide: a process of walking according to the spirit, as Hannah did, in which she learned the proper and powerful use of connection and the strength and peace of detachment and trust. It is truly the only way to parent fearlessly and impart *true and effective* peace, power, and direction to your kids. Yes, you can instill a knowledge of power and direction in your children in other ways; you can even make them fear you; and it is your choice to do that. And that's what keeps me, as a therapist, working. Choose wisely.

Hopefully, you can avoid some of the pitfalls and insecurities that we so easily fall into by finding a firm foundation now and changing the future for you and your kids in a way that can only be described as "beyond your wildest dreams." I am here to encourage, heal, set free, and inspire. Take my hand and come along for the ride.

Marianne Clyde

PART ONE:
THE BEGINNING

THE SET UP:
THE HAND THAT ROCKS THE CRADLE

Eleven dollars was a lot of money over thirty years ago. As a young mom, I did not go out much and watched my pennies pretty closely. I remember feeding a family of three a few years before that on twenty-five dollars a week, and I was pretty good at it. Now we had grown to a family of four. So, eleven dollars comprised almost half my already-tight food budget.

I went on a day trip with some other young moms to the outlets in Reading, Pennsylvania. I felt free, even though I took my sweet, playful four-year-old daughter, Heather, who loved hiding in the racks of clothes and freaking me out. We were moseying along from shop to shop when we entered a pewter store. There, prominently displayed on a shelf, sat a pewter plate. I could feel electricity travel to my hands and feet as I read the message engraved around its border as if it were written just for me. It read: "The hand that rocks the cradle rules the world."

That's all. But to me, it gave me an identity as "Mom"—a purpose far beyond the backtalk, the temper tantrums, and the frightful hide-and-seek games. To me, it said that I am worthwhile, and that my job determines the course not only of my family and my kids but of the world. It said that *my* hand rules the world, and that what I did every day—among the dirty dishes and family squabbles and rolls of toilet paper strung from the bathroom to the living room—was important and life changing. My heart pumped.

I *so* wanted that plate. I really loved the validation it gave me. But alas, it cost *eleven* dollars. How selfish would I be to buy something so frivolous just to validate myself? I may not have mentioned that I was "the perfectly selfless wife and mother." Of course, this was my own assessment of the situation—not necessarily that of my family. It caused me to put pressure on myself to always do the "right" thing. So, I passed the plate by. I figured that I could get it another time when I had more money.

Needless to say, if you constantly deny yourself in order to appear that you have it all together and have your priorities right, or if you don't say how you feel because you don't want to hurt anyone's feelings or appear to be falling apart, you can imagine that pressure stuffed way down deep as a volcano waiting to erupt—but more on that later.

Over the years, I came to regret the decision not to buy the plate. As I searched, I never could find it anywhere else. (Ever since that time, I advocate buying unique things that really speak to you—even if it is a bit of a stretch.) I never forgot about the plate, never forgot about the message, and never forgot the essential role of parents in shaping young lives. I knew I was raising tomorrow's leaders.

I never for a moment say that I got it right all the time. In fact, I've gotten it wrong a lot. Parenting techniques come and go. Moods rise and fall. Relationships grow and come apart. But

Have you ever seen something unique that spoke to you, but you chose to pass by? Would you do it differently next time?

through it all, I hung onto that truth: The hand that rocks the cradle rules the world.

Years passed quickly—as they tend to do—and my children grew. That four-year-old daughter who hid in the clothing racks on that trip has grown into a thoughtful, caring mom. Over the years, I shared my dream with her. I told her about the plate and its message and how I regretted not buying it. Then, when she was out on her own at about twenty years old—not yet a mom but making a living doing her own thing—I moved to Japan. The first birthday I celebrated after moving to Japan brought a delightful surprise from my daughter: the pewter plate I had seen probably fifteen or sixteen years earlier. I guess you can find anything on eBay! (Of course the price had increased a bit.) So, for the last ten or twelve years, I have had that plate happily hanging on my kitchen wall. My own daughter wanted to validate the thoughts that rang so true to me years before. And now that she is a mom, she proves them true with her own son.

Now I have the opportunity, as well as the platform, from which to share that knowledge and belief with other parents around the world.

The hand that rocks the cradle rules the world. Let it sink in. What does that mean to you? If this is true—and you buy into that belief—how does it alter your thinking? What behaviors need to change? What actions will help you determine how you will reach your goal? And of course, what *is* your goal?

To me, it says that I have to get off the sidelines and get in the game. I have to stop being afraid: afraid of making a mistake, afraid of being judged, afraid of saying how I feel, afraid of not being everything to everyone—just afraid. I have to stop reacting and start acting purposefully in all I do. I have to learn not to let my emotions control my responses; but rather, I must let my responses thoughtfully and proactively align with my goals. Speaking of goals, I need to have some. Where am I headed? If I don't know, I could end up anywhere: a victim of fate or circumstances. And what's worse, so could my kids!

If I did rule the world, what kind of world would I want to create? What goals would I pursue? How would I reach those goals? I am reminded of Mahatma Gandhi, who said, "*Be* the change you want to see in the world." What, after all, *is* the change I want to see in the world? I have to stop living by colloquialisms or catch phrases. I have to learn to define exactly what I want for my life and my kids. I have to be more thoughtful about my life.

As a parent and grandparent, I know that more is caught than taught. Kids learn from our example far more than from our words. So, I have to learn to

> "Be the change you want to see in the world."
> —Mahatma Gandhi

examine my thoughts and behaviors to see if I'd like my kids to imitate me. What qualities and characteristics do I want them to emulate? Which of my characteristics would make me shudder if I saw them copied?

So, reflection is the first step in creating the world I want in order to develop a goal for my own life and ponder the characteristics I want to possess. What environment makes me feel good? How can I create that environment for my family? I have to start paying attention to my own thoughts and feelings. If I get irritated that "nobody ever listens to anybody," I need to understand that listening to and respecting other people is important to me. So how can I change the world with that? I can make an effort to do it myself.

Watching the mindless, mad rush at the holidays and feeling the craziness of the chaos, I understand that I do not want to feel that, nor do I want my family to feel that. So, I can simplify. I can focus on relationships and on doing the things that make sense to me and not fall into the trap of meeting the expectations of a chaotic world.

It's simple, really. I only need to work on developing those characteristics in myself, and then I will *be* what I want to be for my family. I won't have to tell them how to be; they will just feel it, absorb it, and emulate it. I can even enlist their help and ask for their opinions. You know as well as I do that even very small children have opinions. When they feel respected and heard, they emulate the characteristics that make them feel good about themselves. Then, they feel free to create that environment in school and around their friends in their lives. I create my little corner of the world to be good and loving and wholesome and powerful, then my kids create the same in their worlds, and as they grow up, they teach their kids by being rather than by yelling and lecturing. Their kids do the same, and before you know it, I have changed the world.

It all begins with me...and you—today. Let's get started.

An Overview

I've had clients tell me that you shouldn't have to work so hard at a relationship. Marriage shouldn't be this difficult. Parenting is too stressful—really? Once, I heard someone say, "When people complain to me that life is hard, I respond, 'Really? Compared to what?'" Good question. We like to complain; yet, when you think about it, what's the alternative?

Work strengthens muscles—whether the labor is physical, emotional, or spiritual. We all know people who never seem to have to work at anything, and it shows. They have no passion and tend to be pretty shallow. So, let's not complain about how hard life is because we really don't know how hard non-life is. In essence, we have nothing to compare it to, so let's get on with it.

Of course, if you want to accomplish something, you must plan. Whether it's a trip to Paris, a walk to the grocery store, a business, a marriage, raising a child (or two or eight), it takes a plan, and it takes cooperation. If you want to send that child to college someday, that takes a plan too. If you just want to glide along, reacting to things as they come and making decisions on the fly, you will soon have no money, no business, and no relationships. These things take work. Sorry, but that's just the way it is.

> You absolutely have everything it takes to accomplish whatever you want to accomplish right now.

But here's the good news: you absolutely have everything it takes to accomplish whatever you want to accomplish right now. It might take a little discovery and some change, but you've got it all right now. You just need to give it some thought, put things in order, and take the first step.

STEP ONE: DECIDING WHERE YOU ARE HEADED

By what principles do you want to live? What is important to you? What characteristics do you want to embrace? What do you want to think about? How do you want to act? What legacy do you want to leave? These are the questions I started to ask myself that would direct my life. Of course, many possible answers exist, but just think about your own questions for a minute.

Hannah knew what she wanted. She wanted a son, and she wanted that son to grow up to serve God—the same God that proved faithful to her by giving her the child in the first place. She was dead-on focused. She told God what she wanted, and in her self-knowledge and knowledge of her creator, she felt at peace.

What key thing could you possibly do in this world that would have eternal reverberations? If you could focus on one thing for the rest of your life, knowing that this one thing would certainly leave ripples throughout the future and creating an unending legacy so far-reaching that you wouldn't even be able to trace it, would that knowledge fire you up? Would the promise of creating such a bright future inspire you to act? It has inspired me. St. Paul says in Philippians 3:13 and 14, "Brothers, I do not consider myself yet to have taken hold of it. But one thing I do, *forgetting what is behind* and straining toward what is ahead, *I press on toward the goal.*" As with Paul, I feel that we have a high calling in life—one that deserves our unswerving focus and determination, our passion, and our attention.

I believe that the most important work I can do is to help you realize who you really are and recognize the amazing power that dwells within you so that you can make a decision to be a mindful parent, knowing that everything that you do will be etched in the lives of your children. In that way, they, too, become mindful parents, raising mindful children who will become mindful parents all the way through time.

It's not hard, but it does take thought, consistency, patience, and focus. Can it be challenging? Absolutely. Can you do it? That is completely up to you. I will do my part to encourage, lead, and offer resources and support. You just need to commit and follow through.

STEP TWO: DEFINING WHAT YOU WANT

When I consider that we are all connected to the source of life, I then know that we are all connected to each other. Whatever affects me affects you. Whatever hurts me hurts you. Whatever benefits me benefits you. We are one with the creator. We are one with each other. I want to examine what that means and how it plays out.

Good parents share many characteristics. Beginning with Hannah's example of focused faith, I trimmed the list down to ten characteristics that seem to encompass the rest.

THE TEN ESSENTIAL PRINCIPLES OF PEACEFUL PARENTING

Connect to the creator
Know your true identity
Nurture awareness
Breathe
Respect
Practice gratitude
Limit judgments
Detach
Communicate effectively
Forgive quickly

Notice that this list has nothing to do with parenting techniques and everything to do with being the type of person you
would like to be. At least, it has to do with being the type of
person I want to be. You are welcome to join me.

PART TWO:
THE TEN ESSENTIAL PRINCIPLES

PRINCIPLE 1:
CONNECT TO THE CREATOR

"Eye hath not seen, nor ear heard, neither have entered into the heart of man, the things which God hath prepared for them that love him." —I Corinthians 2:9 KJV

If I want to connect with God, I must really get to know who he is. What characteristics does the creator possess? If I am one with him, what does that mean for me? What does that look like? How does that play out in real life? I really want to get away from religious clichés and catch phrases that put this type of thinking in a box of any sort. God, no matter how you perceive him, cannot be put into a box. People experience him differently—even those of the same faith or religion. We all hold unique views of the world, unique perceptions of things, and unique expressions of those things. So, it is important to become curious, to ask questions, and to stop all assumptions about what you know, what you think you know, and what others expect you to know.

> *What characteristics do you associate with God? If you are truly one with Him, those characteristics should be flowing from you as naturally as your breath.*

And thus, I find myself curious about God. The characteristics I associate with him include: love, joy, peace, patience, kindness, goodness, meekness, faithfulness, and self-control—qualities referred to in the Bible as the "fruit of the spirit." These will apparently flow from me if I truly become one with him. I think of other characteristics too: wisdom and creativity, for example. God constantly creates. He constantly moves forward and doesn't look back with regret. He knows all things.

The Bible also says I have the mind of Christ—really? That would mean that I, too, have access to all knowledge. He is the *source* of all things. If that is, in fact, the case, then I have access to all of his abundance, so I never need to worry about provision of any kind.

As I pick these beliefs apart, they may seem difficult to grasp. If I have access to all abundance, then why am I broke? Why am I sick? Why am I lonely? These questions pop up all the time in my counseling sessions. What we have here is a huge disconnect. I regularly have clients who are afraid of "being out of God's will," or wondering why he is punishing them or how he could allow a miscarriage or an accident or some dreadful loss. Do you ever find yourself with these thoughts running through your head? They can be debilitating, depressing, and just plain paralyzing. It is just these kinds of thoughts that cause people to become depressed or to leave faith behind because it just isn't working anymore. We think there must be something wrong with us because we don't seem to get it. This is where many want to give up—or at least come looking for help.

This morning as I meditated and prayed, I seemed to get a picture of what is going on. I will try to articulate it as well as I can. I believe that we share a connection at our very core with the living and active source of life. This connection begins from the moment of creation and is like a flowing stream or river. As we allow that source to flow through us, we flow in love and joy and curiosity: like a young child does.

When we get offended or hurt or angry, it's as if someone tosses a stone into the mouth of that little fountain of joy and stops it up. When we become remorseful or look back at yesterday with regret and longing, we face in the wrong direction and go against that flow. When we marinate in unforgiveness and rage, we stop it up even more until it becomes so clogged that we can't even imagine flowing with love. We feel like we have a right to be angry. We couldn't possibly justify forgiving something so awful. We find ourselves judging others and being critical, and our expectations become more difficult to meet.

Many of these I will address in future chapters. But for now, realize that these behaviors stop the flow—justified or not. You can choose to flow in what refreshes or stay stagnant and begin to stink and attract flies and mosquitoes—and ultimately, disease. For when your spirit is stopped up, your body begins to collect toxins that stagnate and eventually make you sick. It's really all in your hands.

> *Incongruent thoughts and behaviors stop the life-giving flow of love and power that should be bursting forth from you.*

You're right if you think you have the choice whether or not to go against the flow. But boy oh boy, it sure doesn't make sense to me when I can be free. The Bible offers us that choice in several places. Joshua 24:15 says, "Choose this day whom you will serve...." Absolutely, it is up to you. In my opinion, it just makes sense to choose the feeling of freedom and life. It makes sense to choose the refreshment of flow and life as opposed to stagnation and disease.

John 8:36 says, "If the Son sets you free, you will be free indeed." Often, people interpret this as freedom to follow a certain set of rules—freedom to belong to a certain faith. This is not what I am commenting on here. I believe that Jesus came to show us how we can be one with God as he was. When he lived through the power that he knew resided in him (as it resides in you), he was free from fear; free to live a life of purpose and destiny; and free to live a life of victory and purpose. When we join with him, we can embrace that freedom as well. He said he came so that we "might have life and have it abundantly!" (John 10:10) I am all for an abundant life. He shows us the ingredients it takes to live that way. We need to make a choice that we will live this way—every day and in every decision. Do we choose life, or do we choose stagnation and defeat? Do I choose to believe and recognize that I am one with the living God and can flow in his character, or do I choose to swim upstream and struggle with things that are my "right to feel" and end up feeling depressed and sick?

The choice is yours and mine, and, in my opinion, it's pretty clear. Life is a journey not a destination. It is an adventure to be lived and figured out as we go along. Of course, as soon as we think we have it figured out, it changes, or our perspective changes.

Change is just a sign of life, of growth, and of movement. Once the growth and movement stop, so does life. With this in mind, I would encourage each of us to embrace change; get comfortable with it, because it is one of the only constant things in life.

Because change is constant, we can easily find ourselves tossed to and fro with every upheaval. It can feel destabilizing, unsteadying, and frightening. As chaos encircles us, we can easily become dizzy and lose perspective if we don't really know who we are—if we have not really extended our spiritual and emotional roots down deep so we cannot be uprooted. We often get uprooted physically: as we have seen with all the natural disasters in many parts of the world. But with secure spiritual roots, we can hold steady in our true identity.

Even with a strong identity, as long as you think you are doing this on your own or that you are expected to do it on your own, you will fail. The flesh is weak—willing, yes, but weak. We run out of energy and resources, and we have conflicting thoughts and goals. We need the steady flow that comes from being connected to the source of: life, love itself, abundance, creation and creativity, peace beyond understanding, and the wisdom of the universe. We need to stay connected and to figure out a way to remember every day to stay connected: using five minutes to listen to the quiet, taking a deep breath with every challenge, or practicing gratitude in place of complaining.

I took my own advice and lay on the hammock one day, enjoying the shade with bits of sunshine filtering through the vines on the arbor above me. I noticed the tweets from the birds and listened to the gentle bubbling of the waterfall on the pool. I felt vaguely aware of the puppies running around, playing, and chasing each other. Every now and then, one would stop by and stick a cold nose on my hot skin, just to say, "I love you, Mom." Dreamily grateful and connected with God, I felt very aware that he surrounds me and abides in me, and that I am one with all this tranquility.

Out of nowhere, I was startled by rustling, barking, and loudly chirping birds. I spilled off my perch and immediately saw the terrified little sparrow that had fallen out of his nest and with whom my puppies wanted to play. Unless someone (I) intervened, his short life would end. Quickly, I grabbed one dog by the collar, chased down the other (kind of tough with one already in tow, but I managed), and spirited them away from the terrified bird and its mama, who'd swooped in to save her offspring. Both birds survived the onslaught, and for a split second, all I could think was, *so much for my communing with God!*

But wait, maybe I did. I saved a life. Maybe I was one with God after all.

Clearly, maintaining that connection to God is not only vital for you but others as well. It just doesn't always appear as you would expect. Enjoy your days of chaos; just stay plugged in, and the creator will lead you where you need to go.

If we can remain steady and secure emotionally and spiritually, we can stay grounded—no matter what happens. Having said that, I come to the questions: "How can I do that? How can I find out who I really am? How do I become really grounded? What is my true identity?" So that makes my next "want" very clear. I want to discover my true identity.

Principle 2:
Know Your True Identity

"...That you may be perfect and complete, lacking in nothing."
—James 1:4
"But the person who unites himself with the Lord becomes one spirit with him." —1 Corinthians 6:17
"You have your being within the Creator, and are all sparks of God. You are indestructible...."

—St. Germain (quoted from lightparty.com)

If I can discover my true identity, I can begin to see how I fit into this world. I must learn to notice what is around me and how it affects me—not to mention how I affect it. So often, we function in life from a locus of control outside of ourselves. We allow what happens to us to control us—similar to being blown around in a windstorm, feeling as if we have no control over anything.

By identifying who we really are and becoming grounded in that knowledge, we develop an internal locus of control: a sense within us that there are things that we can control. We can control our thoughts, our perceptions, the questions we ask, the words we say, the things we do, and the energy we put out. Anything that comes from within us, we control.

> By identifying who we really are and becoming grounded in that knowledge, we develop an internal locus of control, a sense within us that there are things that we can control. We can control our thoughts, our perceptions, the questions we ask, the words we say, the things we do, and the energy we put out. Anything that comes from within us, we control.

Yes, you are your child's mom or dad. Perhaps you are someone's wife or husband. You might have a career as a therapist, a doctor, a librarian, a teacher, a lawyer, a receptionist, a park ranger, or a politician. You could be tall, skinny, short, fat, pretty, plain; prone to anxiety or bipolar; the child of alcoholics; or a preacher's kid. You might be popular or a loner. All these things might be true, but they do not define you, and they can all change. They can all be taken away.

It seems the stories that we find most heartbreaking and which hit home so powerfully are the ones in which a parent loses a child. That type of loss could send you spiraling into despair or utterly destroy you if you were not completely sure of your true identity and the character of God.

Just two days ago, as of this writing, the news resounded with the devastation of the shooting of twenty children and seven adults at the Sandy Hook Elementary School in Connecticut. A story like that can feel like a sucker punch—whether you live nearby or far away. I have received e-mails from people as far away as Japan expressing their grief. The ripples of such evil and devastation travel far. Does this shake up your world? Absolutely.

And yet, the dad of one of the victims began to regain his footing because he had a secure idea of both his identity and his daughter's. He didn't jump on the "hate" bandwagon toward the shooter because he understood who he was and that the family of the shooter felt just as devastated over losing their child as he felt over losing his. To heap hatred on top of that would serve no purpose except to fuel more hatred and instability. Instead, he chose to remember his daughter, Emily, how delightfully she lived her short life, and how blessed he felt to be her dad.

This by no means minimizes his heartache and pain, but it puts him on firmer footing for healing. It minimizes the poison that shoots through the spirit—the hatred that might threaten the stability of the community and cause disease and continued devastation rather than movement toward wholeness once again. He is choosing "The road less travelled...," as Robert Frost would say, and that makes all the difference.

It sounds to me (as an observer) like he was close to his daughter, proud of her, and grateful for her young life. It also sounds to me like he was able to separate from some of the unstable things on which many choose to base their identities, such as: possessions, position, power, or reputation. If you stand on any of these unstable things to describe yourself, you are standing on a fault line that could shift and take your identity with it. Then, what do you do?

I recently read an article about a mom whose twenty-three year old son was killed by a drunk driver. He had been her precious son—her diving buddy. She had wrapped up much of her identity in their relationship. His death devastated her. Paralyzed, she just couldn't get past the gut-wrenching grief of losing him. The paralysis lasted years, until she started worrying about her sanity.

Through therapy, she found a way to detach her identity from the grief. As heartbreaking as losing a child can be, the tragedy is compounded if you also lose yourself in the process. She was able to strengthen her core: her sense of her true self. Once she did this, she could grieve for her son and let him go—as sad as that was. She, of course, will never forget him and never stop loving him, but she can now go on living without allowing the circumstances of her life to alter her identity.

And then there might be the case of the little bundle who shows up all of a sudden—pink and sweet and desperately needy. You had longed for another child, and your son is old enough now to really appreciate a new sibling and enjoy the responsibility, the company, and the new member of the family. But this new bundle isn't really yours. She may be one day; you never know. She is in your care because, though her parents love her and want her back, they are struggling right now. Yes, you might get to adopt her one day, but reuniting her with her original family would, of course, be optimal.

How can you give her your full heart and not have it ripped out if she returns to Mom and Dad?

By knowing your true identity and hers.

I have heard parents tell their children that they own them—as a control measure. That kind of statement comes from someone who is not really secure in his or her identity. The truth is you can never own another human being. He or she is not yours to own any more than the sun or wind or rain is yours to own. Even the property we live on, in reality, was created by God. We are borrowing it, enjoying it, harvesting the crops, mowing the grass, trimming the bushes, planting flowers, cultivating it, making it even more beautiful, and increasing its value. But owning it—really? It's the same with a child.

If you know in your heart that you are already whole, perfect, and complete and are here to share your gifts and to help make the world a better place by contributing your true self, then you can offer all the love you have to another human being without needing anything back. That kind of knowledge helps set the stage for children to know that they are also complete and that love is not finite—not a commodity to be traded for goods, services, or even feelings. It just is. Like other energies, it is limitless if it is allowed to flow freely, and it will come back to you if you just let it fly its own path.

You need to form your identity around what is changeless, timeless, strong, and true. You are a child of the living God. His breath and life are inside you. Because he is, you are whole, perfect, complete, and lacking nothing. That never changes.

We often feel overwhelmed by circumstances, thrown off guard by a thoughtless statement, offended, and unappreciated. I can help keep you from going there. It's important to consider what you *can* do. What *do* you have control over? In such a devastating moment such as losing what or whom you cherish unexpectedly, it's best to have no regrets.

One of the best ways to do this is to become mindful—purposeful—about your life. Take the time to think about what matters to you and live as if it does. Make time with your child and others important to you so that when something does happen, you are not left wringing your hands, wishing you had done more. When you live your life purposefully, you will leave fewer questions unanswered, words unspoken, or dreams unrealized.

I try to remember that rule each time I leave one of my loved ones; I want them to know that I love them and cherish them. That means no mumbling under my breath as I walk out the door about what jerks they are, no name-calling or accusations that they will never amount to anything, no sighs about "always" and "never," and no unaddressed anger or disappointment. I have only the recurring thought that I may be leaving them for the last time, so how do I want them to remember our relationship? Do I want lingering doubts and frustrations left to roll around in their minds? Would I ever—for one moment—want my kids to wonder if I really loved them? Of course not; so my words and actions continually prove that I do.

I understand that these are lofty goals and difficult to *always* remember, but certainly they are worthy of keeping in mind and considering on a regular basis. If you fail, don't throw away the goal—just keep it in mind for next time. In doing this, you will have more "next times" that feel good than those that don't, until you get to the point when there is no next time. I don't say that to be depressing or dark, just to encourage each of us to be aware—myself included.

My dad lives in a nursing home as of this writing. My siblings and I recognize the importance of not harboring any regrets about his care. We do not judge each other about the frequency or intensity of our visits, as we all come from different areas. We each go whenever we can, do whatever we can, and meet to discuss his care and progress whenever possible. There are no judgments: just purposeful action as each sees fit. I don't have to live up to others' expectations of what I *should* be doing—just my own.

This is another important factor in knowing your identity. Other people will have opinions and expectations and ideas. That's great. There is wisdom in many counselors, according to Proverbs. However, there comes a point when you have to do what you need to do. You have to be who you are—no matter what everyone else thinks. You will find no shortage of people's opinions. Use them for what they are: information. And just as you use any information, give more weight to what you consider credible and then make a decision based on what you think is best.

As you can see by the examples in this chapter, we never have tomorrow in our pockets—just today. So the real question is: What are you going to do today? The better you live the present moment, the happier and more peaceful any tomorrows might be. The more completely you can give of yourself, the more opportunities will arise for you to strengthen and increase all that you are.

In living our own completeness, we can be so much more valuable to everyone else—particularly the children in our lives. When they feel secure in their identities, they won't be thrown into a tizzy when someone disagrees with them or criticizes them. These secure identities will know who they really are and allow others to have opinions; they will love others without owning them or sucking the energy from them or making them feel guilty if they need to go their own way.

> In living our own complete-ness, we can be so much more valuable to everyone else—particularly the chil-dren in our lives.

A secure identity reminds you that you are valuable and complete and gifted and unique—no matter what anyone else says or does. At your very core, this is who you are. No matter what storms come, you are as calm and quiet and strong as the eye. Nothing can touch you, and nothing can change that. Remember that and breathe it in.

If you are not clear and secure in your own identity, you may be tempted to try to discover your identity through your child. Picture for a moment that dad at the T-ball game swearing at his five-year-old because his tentative little swing missed the ball perched on the tee again. He's all bent out of shape, taking his frustration out on his child, and for what reason? Perhaps it's because *he* never achieved his life-long dream of making the big leagues; but you can darn well be sure that his *son* will get there, if he has anything to do with it. It sure would be sad if his son were, in fact, destined to grow up to be a very gifted writer or actor or inventor because Dad has blinders on that can only see his son fulfilling his own lost dreams. In being short-sighted like this, Dad is clearly derailing his son from his true identity, most surely creating a tension between them and within his son's psyche that will be difficult to repair—ever. I think we can all pull up a picture in our minds of a parent like this. Just make sure it isn't you.

Being a mindful parent has nothing to do with a second chance to live your dreams but has everything to do with making this moment count for you and your child. It means detaching from your preconceived notions and accepting your child for who he or she is—not who you wish he or she was. It means embracing "what is" and being grateful for that. In doing that, you also teach your child the life-enriching skills of observation, acceptance, and gratitude—which leads us to the next principle for peaceful parents: nurturing awareness.

PRINCIPLE 3:
NURTURE AWARENESS

"The ultimate value of life depends upon awareness and the power of contemplation rather than upon mere survival."
—*Aristotle*

Some people feel confused about how to practice the presence of God. Some might think it means that you have to be religious; others might think it sounds pretty complicated, or rigid, or strange. In reality, it's none of those things. It's a matter of nurturing awareness. If God created everything out of nothing, then we really are connected with everything and everyone and are one with all things. So technically, it encompasses a process of getting to know ourselves and our environment and what exists around us. It's fun, relaxing to do, and easy to teach your kids. You can experience it together.

Let the awareness of God be a natural part of your day. A walk in the woods can turn into a listening exercise and a lesson in mindfulness. "Let's count how many kinds of birds we hear." "Let's be still and see if we can hear a deer approaching." "Can you smell the leaves and flowers?" "Can you taste the honeysuckle?" Kids can have a fun, eye-opening experience tasting herbs in the garden. They can treat themselves to the surprising sweetness of stevia leaves, the soothing taste of spearmint, or the pungent flavor of basil leaves.

To calm down and relax, you can lie on your back in the grass and point to the different cloud shapes. "What does that look like to you?" Watch the tadpoles in the brook; feed the fish in the pond; watch the ants; listen to the wind—what does it say to you? It's amazing how a child's short attention span can be intrigued and expanded by such things.

Making the time to listen and practice awareness can increase children's patience by teaching them to sit still longer. You can sit on a log and count the ants or sit on a bridge or a creek bank with fishing nets and catch minnows. Trying to cross a shallow stream on a log can help with balance and coordination. I find that it helps me too. Many times, my grandson will turn around and reach for my hand and say, "Here Grandma, I'll help you. It's okay." I get my turn to pull him up the steep banks as well. It's a great way to teach cooperation and interdependence.

The other day, he and I were driving in the car when a young bear crossed the road in front of us. What a thrill! "He's looking at us!" "What do you think he's thinking?" "How old do you think he is?" The little bear seemed as curious about us and we were of him. Be ready for those moments. We had prayed to see a bear a couple of weeks prior—what a cool way to remind my grandson that God hears him. We always look for wildlife: deer, turkeys, foxes, or

> *Teach your children to always look for the little miracles of life in their everyday experiences.*

groundhogs. Awareness creates an alertness and a sensitivity to creation. Teach your children to always look for the little miracles of life in their everyday experiences.

My grandson loves to walk and smell the flowers or to play in a puddle of water in an old tree trunk. He has even been known to hug a tree—not for a political statement, but just for the joy of appreciating creation and the creator.

Teaching your children awareness of their surroundings benefits their safety as well. It will make them aware of where they are, what and who is around them, and what that means for their safety. It will even teach your children to think and create. "How do you think the bear feels without his mom nearby?" They can learn empathy and awareness of others' feelings too. We so often pull a dead frog out of the pool, that my grandson regularly wants to check the skimmers to see if we can save one before it dies.

How many times have you driven toward the ocean and rolled down the windows as you drew near, inhaling the fragrance of the sea and smelling the salt air and the fish? These are the types of things that call up fond memories of my own childhood, so obviously, they last for a long time. When our own children were small and we were blending families, we enjoyed having treasure hunts at the beach. We would send our kids looking for little crabs or seashells, seaweed, and rocks. They had fun gathering all the things on their lists and winning prizes at the dollar store. They could each win in different categories, and then we would have a shopping spree—each feeling excited about his or her accomplishments. We, as parents, could feel good about the way they appreciated each other's accomplishments and learned cooperation and awareness at the same time.

You can accomplish so many different things in such quiet, unrushed times or even with fun competitions among kids. You show your kids that they are important enough to spend quality time with you. You teach them valuable skills, such as: listening, paying attention, being still, observing, and practicing awareness—as well as an appreciation of God and nature. You teach them the excitement, too, that exists in their surroundings.

These skills prove so useful; and yet, with all the technology kids use today, their attention spans and listening skills suffer. We label them ADHD and put them on meds. Not that there is anything wrong with progress or medication when it's really needed, but we need to practice a purposeful awareness of our world in teaching kids the art of observation, appreciation, and mindfulness so we can all experience life to the fullest. Leading into the next principle, it all boils down to: "just breathe."

Principle 4:
Breathe

"Breath is the bridge which connects life to consciousness, which unites your body to your thoughts."
—*Thich Nhat Hanh*

It sounds too simple to actually be helpful, but conscious breathing benefits us so significantly that if I could give just one word of advice to someone, it would be: "breathe." Use this technique yourself and teach it to your kids. It's easy, quick, and simple to understand. In the middle of a tantrum, remind your child to take a deep breath. In the middle of your own tantrum, remind yourself to do the same.

Sammy screamed because he wasn't getting his way. He felt angry, hurt, and disappointed and was coming unglued. Mom's first reaction (as it would be for most parents) was to scream back and maybe shock him into shutting up. Does that work? Sometimes. But what does it teach Sammy? It teaches him that screaming is an effective and powerful tool of communication.

Now, my guess is that Mom wasn't thinking about the message she communicated. She only wanted him to be quiet and knock it off. A knee-jerk, reactive parent wants to accomplish her immediate goal and doesn't give a whole lot of thought to her response to the situation until the next time she's driven to such a reaction again. The next time, however, Sammy will be armed with the knowledge (through his previous experience) not only that yelling works effectively, but that when you yell louder and more violently, you win. So now, Mom finds that her tool doesn't work as well, and she hauls off and hits him. The good news? The behavior stops. The bad news? Sammy has learned another effective communication tool: physical violence.

Mom does not understand that she is actually teaching her son how to defy her and get his way. There will most likely come a day when he grows bigger than she is, and she will have no effective way of communicating with her out-of-control son. By that time, he will try out these communication tools with his teachers, classmates, and perhaps anyone else in authority.

We need to remember that we are constantly teaching our kids. We do not have to sit down with them to read a book or hold up flash cards to educate them. They pay more attention to our behavior and the way we do things than any planned activity designed to teach. So we must realize that by every word, action, attitude, and reaction, we mold our kids into the adults they will become.

Which brings us back to the importance of breathing: If we can take a deep breath before we say or do anything and simply remind ourselves that this moment counts, we have an opportunity to convey important information; that momentary pause to breathe can actually save our kids' lives. And who knows how much future heartbreak we might save ourselves?

If we go back to the original situation of Sammy pitching a fit and take a deep breath, we can see several things happening: Sammy is experiencing some strong emotions that he does not know how to handle, and he is asking Mom for help. Maybe you are thinking, "Wait, I didn't see where he asked her for anything. I just heard him screaming." Well, if you just take things at face value (kids making a lot of noise and acting disrespectfully), you might typically respond to chaos and loud negative feelings by shutting them down as quickly and possible. Why? Because so often we feel uncomfortable with chaos and negative feelings—whether they originate in others or in ourselves. We don't like the feeling that comes from the lack of control stirring in us and the resultant negative emotions that rise up. So, our first impulse is to squash it all.

The mindful parent, on the other hand, takes a moment to: breathe deeply, recognize the negative feelings in herself, understand that they are nothing to fear, and allow the feelings to wash over her and dissipate so that she can see clearly the true issue: a child who, beneath the tantrum, wants to learn how to feel better. With a clear mind, she can hear the unspoken questions: Do you love me? Am I worthy? Can you help me?

A parent who only reacts with the fight-or-flight instinct of, "Oh my God! Negative emotions! Noise! Chaos! Out of control! Fire! Grab the hose and let 'em have it!" may, in fact, put out the fire, but he or she has answered each of those unspoken questions with a resounding, "No!" You may not intend to say that. You may argue with, "Of course, I love my child." However, more important than what you *intend* to communicate or what you think everyone should *assume* you are communicating, is how your child actually *interprets* what you have communicated. *That* is what he or she will address in therapy years later—not your intention or assumptions. He or she will carry his or her interpretation of your communication into his or her other interactions, relationships, and view of himself or herself—heavy, but true.

Doesn't that, in itself, make it worth pausing for a moment to "just breathe"?

My Top Five Benefits of Deep Breathing:

1. *It reduces tension in the body.*
2. *It brings clarity to the mind.*
3. *It reduces pain.*
4. *It calms the emotions.*
5. *It releases toxins.*

Deep breathing offers many benefits. Here are my top five.

1. It reduces tension in the body.

    Deep breathing is one of the simplest yet most effective stress management techniques. You can do it anywhere, at any time. It becomes even more effective with practice. Deep breathing works both to prevent harmful reactions to stress and to help relieve them. If you practice deep breathing for a few minutes each day, you'll find that events don't upset you as much as before. Also, whenever you do feel upset, anxious, or worried, taking a few slow, deep breaths can help break the stress cycle and calm you down. Even when you can't control the situation, you can always control your breathing and thus help to change your reaction to those circumstances. [Taken from *Dr. Dean Ornish's Program for Reversing Heart Disease.*]

2. It brings clarity to the mind.

    Many claim that by focusing on your breath—in and out—you can gain enlightenment. According to Dr. Andrew Weil:

    By paying attention to your breath, you will rapidly change your state of consciousness, begin to relax, and slowly detach from ordinary awareness. Try to focus on the point between your in breath and out breath that is dimensionless and glimpse the elements of enlightenment in that space. [Taken from "The Science and Art of Breathing," DrWeil.com.]

3. It reduces pain.

Dr. Debra Fulghum Bruce, co-author of *The Fibro-myalgia Handbook,* says that:

Deep abdominal breathing actually alters your psychological state, making a painful moment diminish in intensity...Researchers know that the brain makes its own morphine-like pain relievers, called endorphins and enkephalins. These hormones are associated with a happy, positive feeling and can help relay 'stop pain' messages throughout your body. During deep abdominal breathing, you will oxygenate your blood, which triggers the release of endorphins while also decreasing the release of stress hormones and slowing down your heart rate.

It is said that said that when adults cut their breathing rates in half—from a normal rate of twelve to eighteen breaths per minute to as low as six per minute—their pain lessened.

4. It calms the emotions.

Did you know that when you get angry, you lower your IQ? Studies have shown that stress and negative emotions (such as anger, fear, and hostility) literally lower your intelligence. The blood rushes *from* your brain to your arms and legs and puts you in fight-or-flight mode. In that mode, your body focuses on survival—not what's best for all involved. When you take a deep breath, hold it for a few seconds, and let it out, you allow oxygen to nurture your vital organs—

including your brain—and bring your body back to full thinking mode, where you can actually see the bigger picture and think reasonably.

If you experience strong emotions, breathing will help them to pass over and beyond you like a wave and level out. A deep breath will give you a moment to think before you speak. It offers a little oasis in the middle of a stressful day.

5. It releases toxins

The body releases a majority of toxins through proper breathing. When we don't breathe deeply from the diaphragm, we create an environment in our bodies that can breed diseases, like: cancer, heart disease, high blood pressure, and even asthma. Lack of oxygen keeps the body's immune system from working properly.

Probably more than anything, breathing connects you to the breath of life—from where all good things originate—and helps you get in touch with the real, calm, peaceful, and loving you. In many cultures, the word for breath and spirit are the same. So, when you focus on breathing or breath, you enter the spiritual realm and remove your thoughts from the limiting physical world.

Taking a moment to breathe before reacting teaches your kids that you don't have to respond in the moment. You don't have to *react*; you can be proactive and choose your responses, your actions, and your words; you can choose to allow the strong emotions to pass.

> *Taking a moment to breathe before reacting teaches your kids that you don't have to respond in the moment.*

Even Dr. Andrew Weil agrees that breathing is a perfect remedy for most things. Just breathe. Of course, when you take a moment to breathe, it allows you to step back and realize the importance of respecting yourself enough to control your strong emotions and to afford others that same courtesy. Respect is the next tool in your peaceful parenting tool kit.

PRINCIPLE 5:
RESPECT

"A person's a person no matter how small." —Dr. Seuss
"Self-respect leads to self-discipline. When you have both
firmly under your belt, that's real power."
—Clint Eastwood

Respect is vital to realizing harmony in the home. As with anything else, if you try to teach something to

> More is caught than taught!

your children, you must first realize it in yourself. Respect yourself and model that for your children so they can see what it looks like. "More is caught than taught," as they say, so you must demonstrate the behavior you want to see.

You and your spouse must respect yourselves and each other. You demonstrate this by never talking badly about yourself or your spouse and by acting kindly to yourself and your spouse.

You must value each opinion—even if you don't agree with it. You must give each individual the space to express his or her opinions and emotions. You must recognize and value boundaries. You must value people over things (including electronic communication). You should use eye contact and full-face attention on a regular basis—rather than yelling from room to room.

You can start when your child is very young by respecting your infant—yes, that's right: your infant. Validate his need to connect. Validate your infant's need to feel important. Talk to him —not just in baby talk and cooing—but as another human being. Explain to him what you are doing when you give him a bath, change his diaper, and walk the floor. Tell your baby you understand that he is unhappy and unable to sleep, reassuring him that you are there, and that it's okay to relax and go back to sleep. Talk in a calm, gentle, soothing voice. Look into your infant's eyes. Let him know that even though he is tiny, you hear and understand his needs—or at least that you will try your best to figure them out. When you rush your baby around and treat him as an object to be washed and fed and changed, you miss a vital opportunity to lay a foundation of connection that both you and he will desperately need in later years when his peer group comes calling. If that tiny little baby does not feel validated and connected to you, he will seek validation elsewhere—and he will get it.

The same principle works with your older children and your spouse. Don't just rush around mindlessly—communicate. Of course, I will address this further in the communication section later in the book, but for now, understand that when you are in a room, even just watching TV, and you get up to leave, you create an empty spot; others wonder what you are doing and where you are going and why you left. Keep in mind that others see the world through their own lenses. Very often, if you don't say anything, others will think you are angry or annoyed with them. A simple "I'll be right back," or "I need to check on the baby," or "I think I am going to go take a shower" all check that fear before it can arise. It provides a simple acknowledgement of the other people in the room.

Another overlooked way to show respect is by allowing others to try and fail and try again—without you stepping in to fix things. When your daughter reaches for something and can't get it, help her figure out a way: don't just reach up and get it for her, even if she starts to whine or cry. Validate her frustration and then ask what else she might try to help solve this dilemma. If your daughter doesn't know or is too upset to think, offer suggestions, such as: "Is there anything you might be able to stand on?" This frees her to remember the stool in the bathroom that she can run and get. The child has then solved her problem, giving her a sense of pride and accomplishment. These little interactions add together to create a sense of competence—if you respect your daughter enough to allow her to figure things out on her own.

So often, we (as parents) think we have to rush in and fix things. We don't want our kids to struggle or feel upset. We may not feel comfortable with tears or anger, so we think we can help by getting them to stop. It's much more respectful to acknowledge their feelings—not shame them for their feelings but allow them to experience them and to move beyond them. It's too easy to respond, "Don't you dare yell at me!" than to say, "Wow, you're pretty angry right now. I know this is hard. I love you. Let's take some deep breaths and talk about it." In the latter case, you will do several things with just that simple statement: You will validate the frustration and teach that feelings are not bad; you will show respect by not flying off the handle; you will model self-control; you will affirm the safety of your love, even in the midst of strong emotions; you will teach a simple de-escalation technique that is easy to use anywhere; and, last but not least, you will suggest that other ways exist to handle anger—not bad for one interaction!

On the other hand, if you say, "Stop being a brat. You are always a drama queen. Get over it," you lay a totally different foundation. You teach your child that getting angry is wrong and unacceptable—that when she has a strong emotion, she misbehaves and overreacts, which means the child cannot competently handle the situation properly. When you tell your child to get over it—with your words or attitude—she gets angrier on the inside, even if she calms down on the outside; she ends up just stuffing her feelings, only to explode at a later time. This is because the one person in the world she thought would or should understand—doesn't. Not only does this invalidate her but it comes across as a withdrawal of love. It paves the way for your child to get validation from that boyfriend or girlfriend you don't like. Every interaction like this drives a wedge between you. If you tell a very young child not to be a crybaby, the same thing happens inside: the child learns that strong emotions are bad, and that he or she is bad. Now the child holds a new identity of "crybaby" and will find something else to calm him or her down next time; it just won't be you.

"Sticks and stones may break my bones, but words will never hurt me!" While that may be a fun rhyme and a nice thought, it's totally wrong. As many of my clients can attest, labels and names attached to them in childhood laid the foundation for a lack of respect they feel for themselves now and provided the reason they readily accept disrespect from others. "I am a loser." "I never get anything right." "I'll never amount to anything." "I'm an idiot." "I'm irresponsible." Do any of these sound familiar? They all start in childhood. Whether the name-calling is by a parent, sibling, or teacher, it doesn't matter. The wound cuts just as deep and feels just as true. Name-calling should never be allowed, and parents should resist labeling kids. The cute one, the smart one, the athletic one—yes, each kid has strengths and weaknesses, but that does not define who they are.

Teaching kids self-respect starts by realizing that just because they're small doesn't mean they don't have something to offer, including strong feelings and opinions. Just because they are small does not mean they will never remember how you spoke to them. This is a huge fallacy that many people still believe. Just because your mind may not readily recall an event doesn't mean it's not there somewhere, subconsciously controlling your life as an adult. Kids must be validated by their parents and must also be taught to value their siblings just as much.

I recently saw a picture of two of my grandsons who fell asleep with their arms resting on each other—not because they were told to, but because their parents took the time and energy to teach their kids to love and respect each other. And it rubs off. The kids feel more secure in their home, and as a result, more secure in the world. Teaching kindness and respect is important in dealing with family members as well as those outside the home, not because everyone "deserves" it, but because it's who you are. In doing so, you create a secure springboard for your children to launch themselves into the unknown. Those are the kids who will be less likely to make unwise choices or to be dragged along with the crowd. When children have been taught to respect themselves and others, they are more comfortable doing what they know is right.

> Dr. John Gottman's Four Biggest Predictors of Divorce
> Contempt
> Criticism
> Defensiveness
> Stonewalling

I often have clients who come to me distressed because their kids slam doors, scream that they hate them, and constantly challenge, manipulate, and speak rudely and disrespectfully. I am not surprised, then, when I hear that Mom and Dad have a challenging relationship, undercutting each other's authority or dismissing each other in front of the kids like one or the other is an idiot. According to Dr. John Gottman (the nation's leading researcher on marriage, divorce, and parenting), showing contempt is more than just a very common form of disrespect. It is also one of the greatest predictors of divorce—along with criticism, defensiveness, and stonewalling. These don't just break up marriages; they tear families apart. It's worth taking a few moments to address each of these issues so that, if you recognize them in your own relationships, you can take steps now to start replacing them with healthier behaviors.

CONTEMPT

Contempt rears its ugly head when one spouse feels superior to the other. I have had many clients whose spouses put them down constantly or ridicule them in front of their kids. Sometimes, this doesn't even happen verbally, but physically: through body language. When a wife rolls her eyes, either to her husband or to others, she says, in essence, that the guy is an idiot. When a husband snorts as his wife tries to explain her dream, he, in effect, says that her ideas are stupid. The wife who constantly puts her husband down, who rolls her eyes at his jokes, who hates hearing his stories over and over again, and then acts devastated and self-righteous when she discovers that he's been unfaithful, needs to take some responsibility for possibly having played some role in the downward spiral of the marriage. Marital troubles do not happen in a vacuum any more than discipline problems do.

We will address the importance of not judging others in a later chapter, but for now, you can see how coming from a place of superiority can ruin a marriage.

CRITICISM

It is certainly normal to disagree about things with your spouse and even to voice complaints, but when the criticism becomes personal, it's time to reassess. "I am embarrassed that we are always late," has quite a different effect than, "You are always late; you make me look bad!"

"A cluttered house makes me feel anxious and fidgety" is a complaint. "You are a dreadful housekeeper" is criticism. "You never listen to me" is criticism. "I feel unheard when you don't stop what you are doing to listen to what I am saying" is a complaint. "Can't you do anything right?" is criticism; "I get frustrated when you don't do what I ask you to do" is a statement in which the speaker takes responsibility for his or her feelings.

Can you hear the difference? One type of communication can put a deep wedge between spouses, destroy a relationship, and devastate self-esteem. The other type consists of straightforward statements in which the speaker takes responsibility for his or her own feelings by stating them clearly. This limits the perceived need for defensiveness on the part of the listener and opens the door for a mindful, respectful response.

Confrontation is often difficult and uncomfortable, but by approaching it respectfully and without criticism, you can more easily resolve the issues at hand.

DEFENSIVENESS

I see families all the time who employ criticism and defensiveness as regular modes of communication. The natural reaction when someone criticizes you is to defend yourself. Your stress hormones get released, and you go into fight-or-flight mode. Your brain says, "You're in danger; you'd better fight back!" Somewhere in this cycle, someone must step back, take a deep breath, and say to himself or herself, "I am not in danger; this person obviously has a problem and didn't express it very well. I am able to hear past the delivery and validate the emotion so we can find a resolution."

People spend a great deal of time in relationships proving that one person is right and the other is wrong. It does not have to be this way. Everyone does not have to agree with your opinions. The kids do not have to agree with your decisions. You usually have no need to defend them. If you are right, you are right. Proving it will not make you any "righter." And proving yourself right and your spouse or your child wrong only creates the environment of winners and losers. It often works better if you just say, "You might be right, but in this case, I think this is the best decision. Maybe you are right, but at the moment this is how I feel."

Or if someone respectfully disagrees with your decision or opinion, you will be more likely to willingly hear their input. Children need to learn that they'll get better results and more cooperation when they act respectfully.

STONEWALLING

Sometimes you need to cool down when a discussion gets too heated. Sometimes you need to walk away for a few minutes. These are beneficial tools in communication. The problem comes when one of you says, "Whatever!" or "Fine!" and shuts down. If you need to walk away, politely say, "I don't feel like we are getting anywhere right now; can we pick this conversation back up in the morning?" Another option is to recognize your emotions. "I'm just getting angry and can't hear you right now. Let's take a thirty-minute break and try again." Or go for a short walk to relieve tension (but always say when you will return).

By slamming shut or "stonewalling," you in essence tell your child or spouse that they are not worth any more of your time. Certainly, if they act disrespectfully and harangue you, the conversation needs a break until they can approach you in a respectful manner.

If you see these patterns operating in your home, change them immediately—even if you have to have a family meeting to address the problem and set up new rules about respect. But make sure that you don't demand certain behaviors from your children that you and your spouse are unwilling to practice yourselves. If you have a spouse who cannot seem to act respectfully, that does not mean you have to react in kind. You can always control your attitude. You can always control what comes out of your mouth. You can always practice kindness. And you can't change someone who refuses to change. These are all valuable lessons to teach your children, and allowing your children to see you living these truths is the most effective teaching technique. So respect yourself enough to take care of yourself and manage your own strong feelings effectively as a gift to yourself and your kids.

Whatever you focus on, you will attract into your life. If you focus on what is wrong and what is not working, you will only attract more of it into your life. Stay focused on what you *can* do. Stay focused on what you put out there. If you put out love and respect, you will draw love and respect to you. Our next principle emphasizes that point: gratitude. When you give thanks for what you have, you will attract more of it.

Principle 6:
Practice Gratitude

"Finally, brothers, whatever is true, whatever is noble, whatever is right, whatever is pure, whatever is lovely, whatever is admirable—if anything is excellent or praiseworthy—think about such things." —Philippians 4:8
"...In everything give thanks...."—1 Thessalonians 5:18

My hands were full: juggling groceries, my purse, my four-year-old grandson's backpack, and my briefcase. The little guy followed along behind as I struggled to get the garage door open and walk through the breezeway to the house. "Grandma, what's that?" he asked, pointing to the Christmas wreath I had hurriedly put together—just because I thought I ought to get *some* holiday decorations up. I said, "Oh that's a Christmas wreath I made," not thinking much of it. He just stood there, eyes glued on the wreath. "Wow, Grandma, thanks for doing that." It made my day. His thoughtful, innocent, truly grateful response to something I slapped together melted my heart. He thanked me as if I carefully and thoughtfully created a masterpiece just for him. That kind of spontaneous, observant gratitude does wonders to cement a relationship.

> Spontaneous, observant gratitude does wonders to cement a relationship.

What would happen to our relationship with God and each other if we truly saw each act, however small or ordinary, as a masterpiece—a reason for recognition and gratitude? What if we looked at each little blossom as if it were a gift just for us at that moment? How would our relationships change if each family member really appreciated the contributions of the others—however small? Maybe those contributions would not remain small for long. Each person longs for validation and affirmation. We all want to be noticed and appreciated for who we are and what we do. While God doesn't need our affirmation for his own validation, according to his laws of nature, the universe responds to it by multiplying positivity.

> What you bring into focus in your life, you talk about, you think about, and you end up drawing to you.

Practicing gratitude places the focus clearly on what you have as opposed to what you don't have. There are many reasons we are encouraged to do this. For starters, whatever you concentrate on increases in your life, just as whatever you focus on when you take a picture clearly defines the subject and quality of the photo. What you bring into focus in your life, you talk about, you think about, and you end up drawing to you. If you focus on poverty and bills and lack, you attract more of that. Most people don't realize that they continually communicate with God. You put out your energies, and he answers. The subconscious does not know imagination from reality; it only knows what you think about all the time and how you feel about it. So it figures, if you obsess about your crummy relationship with your spouse, your terribly disobedient children, or your ramshackle house, that must be what you want, and it takes you at your word and sends you more of it.

There's a little saying, "Count your troubles, you'll be sad; count your blessings, you'll be glad." It's rather simple. Instead of always complaining about your disobedient kids, start being thankful for them, for the way they think, for the opportunity to raise them, and for their strong and varied personalities. Rather than worrying about how everything has gone wrong with your house, try to thank God for a roof over your head and concentrate on the charm, the affordable house payment, and the fun you have decorating. And even though your spouse may not be perfect, he or she does have great qualities, and there are surely things that you appreciate about being married. Start being thankful for those things and see how quickly your life seems to change.

The amount of happiness and joy you have in your life is directly related to your ability to acknowledge what you are grateful for. Studies have shown that among the leading characteristics of strong families is the ability to express appreciation: not only for what each does but for who they are.

I recently met with a husband who told me that his new wife changed his life because she expressed her thanks to him for everything, even the small things that we tend to overlook. It has made a huge difference in their marriage—as well as their outlook on life. Even when you are not in the presence of your spouse or kids, talk about them in a positive way. Convey to your friends and coworkers how grateful you feel for them. Your outlook and attitude determine the direction of your life—not the external things that seem annoying or wrong at the moment. You captain your own ship. You determine the course of your life. You are not a victim in any way—unless you choose to put yourself in that role. A victor sees where he or she is going and enjoys the journey. Gratitude helps you get there. As a matter of fact, you can't get there without it. You will keep circling and circling, getting tossed around on the waves you focus on.

This is what happened to Peter in Matthew 14. The wind and waves were crashing all around, but Jesus walked on the water. When Peter wanted to walk on the water, Jesus told him to get out of the boat. For a moment, it seemed like he would be able to do it, but his focus changed from Jesus to the chaos and danger swirling around him, and he began to sink. That's when we begin to go under too. When we take our eyes off of the good and focus on what bothers us, we spin down a spiral of despair that sucks us under.

What you focus on increases. Don't wait, always looking toward the future for what you will be thankful for one day. Be thankful for what you have today. Make a practice of being grateful. Make a mental list before you get out of bed in the morning or before you drift off to sleep at night. Write a gratitude list when you feel overwhelmed and tempted to get anxious or depressed. What *is* working; what *do* you have? Focus on that. It's important to be thankful in all circumstances. Without our trials, we would not grow. Without those challenges with our children, we wouldn't recognize our own weakness. Our spouses and children serve as our best teachers. They show us where we are now and where we still need to go.

You may think that you are fine the way you are: that you don't need to grow. Yet consider the laws of nature. Anything that stops growing is dying. The same goes for you and your relationships. I know it's much more comfortable to just be the way you have always been and do things the way you've always done them, but are you really happy that way? From what I have seen as a therapist, I tend to agree with Henry David Thoreau when he said, "The mass of men lead lives of quiet desperation." Chances are: you are one of them. This need not be true! Start to see things in the encouraging and bright light of gratitude. It takes no time and no special skills, and you can start immediately.

Now you might say, "Yes, but you don't know my situation. My life is filled with troubles. I can't just turn into a 'Pollyanna' and expect them to disappear." All I can say in response to that is that it's up to you. You can stay where you are, but you don't have to. You can always find plenty to be thankful for. And not only will it benefit you to begin this practice, but it will benefit your kids even more because you will teach them to start this practice early in their lives, and their lives will be that much better because of it. So if you don't do it for you, do it for your kids.

Kids who are taught gratitude are less likely to have the "entitlement" mentality that we see so often today. When a child feels content, he or she experiences less stress and resentment, resulting in better overall health. As we all know too well, stress hormones released into the body that have no outlet for release impact your immune system, your heart, and other organs, and they decrease your resistance to disease.

I Love You More Than Rainbows, by Susan Crites, is as excellent book to stir your child's imagination and get him or her thinking about positive things. Since reading the book, my grandson and I often get into a little contest about how much we love each other. I will say, "I love you more than rainbows," and he'll follow with something like, "I love you more than pizza!" Back and forth we go, thinking up things we love and having fun being silly and being positive. It's a great bonding exercise, plus it promotes positive focus and stirs up the thinking process.

Over the years, I have suggested many ways for clients to make gratitude fun and memorable and to strengthen it into a habit. For example, give each of your kids a roll of toilet paper (or paper towels, shelf paper, or whatever you might have handy) and have them fill out each square with things they are thankful for. You can give a little prize to whoever thinks of the most.

A NOTE ABOUT COMPETITION:

Competition is not the enemy. It can be used to spur each other on to greatness. The important thing about competition is to promote good, healthy principles of sportsmanship. Competition can be harmful when used to pit one sibling against the other. "Why can't you be more like your sister?" "David gets good grades; what's wrong with you?" "Annie is definitely the prettier of the two girls." "Dustin is clearly the athlete; Josh seems to only like art. I don't know what to do with him." These statements clearly foster harmful competition, creating a space for kids to feel resentful toward a sibling because Mom obviously prefers one over the other.

Creating a fun atmosphere that nurtures good-natured competition can encourage a child to be the best he or she can be. Games to promote certain characteristics (such as gratitude) can help. Encourage kids to find nice things to say to each other—to express thanks even for the little things. Writing thank-you notes is another way to do this. A couple of my daughters-in-law are particularly good at this and encourage their children to write notes for every gift they receive. Such a habit teaches kids to not only be focused on what they get but to express gratitude to the giver.

Thanking God for all your blessings is so much more pleasant than praying for him to make you well when you get sick; yet, unfortunately, that is what most of us do. We forget to acknowledge the good things in our lives, but when we get in trouble, we run to God and ask him to fix it. Perhaps if we practiced active gratitude for our health, our good appetites, our strong bones and muscles, our prosperity, our skills and talents, and our relationships, we might be less likely to get sick in the first place.

Studies have shown that people who practice gratitude regularly are less likely to show symptoms of depression and experience higher levels of life satisfaction than those who do not. Having higher levels of life satisfaction leads to better quality of sleep, which is important in maintaining a healthy lifestyle. It is obvious that it feels more fulfilling and less stressful to be in a relationship with someone who appreciates you than one in which you feel taken for granted.

Since gratitude leads to greater contentment, you will be less likely to judge others. This leads us to our next principle: limit judgments.

Principle 7:
Limit Judgments

"If you judge people, you have no time to love them."
—*Mother Theresa*
"When people see some things as beautiful, other things become ugly.
When people see some things as good, other things become bad."
—*Lao Tsu*

Slamming on the brakes and laying hard on the horn, Maria screams at the other driver, "What the hell is the matter with you?" Then she growls to herself, "What an idiot," as she gives the guy the finger and then absentmindedly swerves in front of another car. This in turn prompts that driver to pounce on his horn, causing a chain reaction of anger, impatience, and knee-jerk responses from everybody on the road. And we all know what that means: that aggravation will follow everyone involved into their workplaces, their errands, or wherever they're headed. It affects them and all those they encounter.

Frankly, that's not the kind of emotion any of us need to "pay forward."

Maria had no way of knowing that the man who cut her off was watching his son potentially bleed to death in his front seat, and that he was rushing feverishly to get to the hospital in time. His son had accidentally tripped over the dog in his rush to get to school on time and had broken through the sliding glass door.

However, the reason really doesn't matter. Her reaction and judgment toward the man increased his anxiety when his emotional bucket was already full. Her reaction also started her day out on the wrong foot, which in turn put a wet blanket on everyone she came in contact with, and the ripple effects can still be felt to this day. Relationships are ruined. People who didn't do anything wrong feel hurt and invalidated. And on it goes.

It would have felt a whole lot better if she had just let the incident pass without so much as a thought, or even better yet, had sent the other driver a blessing, figuring he might have had something else on his mind. We have all done inconsiderate things. We have all been distracted by daily stressors, big and small. Don't we all want others to give us the benefit of the doubt? Wouldn't we all wish to be the recipient of someone's grace—whether we deserved it or not?

It brings to mind a memory I have of pulling into the first available parking place in front of Walmart one day, not really paying attention. As I began to get out of my car, a man walked up and said (in a sarcastic tone), "That space is for physically handicapped—not mentally handicapped," and kept walking—really? Wouldn't it have been more productive—and just as effective—to say, "Excuse me, did you know you are in a handicap spot?" He could have walked away knowing that he had helped someone and felt good about that. I would have been grateful that he had pointed out what I did not notice and would have thought, "Now, that was nice of him to say something." Everybody would have been happy; everybody would have stayed calm; and everyone would have walked away feeling better. If we have to make assumptions, why can't we each assume that other people are trying their best?

Why is it that we often feel compelled to make other people feel inferior or wrong or stupid? Does that really make us feel better? If that's what we need to feel powerful, needed, or important, it's an indication that we need to work on some things. The other approach is easier and calmer and makes everyone feel better.

The nonjudgmental approach is also healthier for you. If you always harbor negative feelings—and a judgmental attitude indicates this—you are at higher risk for disease. If you constantly live in fight-or-flight mode, you release stress hormones (like adrenaline and cortisol) in excess amounts. When these types of hormones are released in excess or in a chronic way, you become more vulnerable to heart attack and stroke, your immune system becomes compromised, and you can develop memory problems and lessen brain function, creating an atmosphere in your body in which cancer can grow unimpeded. So go ahead and judge if you want to, but it's so much easier on your body to be nice. It makes so much more sense to stop comparing yourself to others all the time and just let people be.

BEING JUDGMENTAL IS DISTRACTING

We all want to be accepted for who *we* are, but we seem less concerned with letting other people be who *they* are. Learn to let it go. Spend your time focusing on where you are headed and what's important to you. Every time you stop to judge someone else, you get derailed from *your* purpose and *your* dream. You are the only one who can follow your path, so why spend your time and effort standing in someone else's?

BEING JUDGED HURTS MORE THAN JUST YOUR FEELINGS

When you base your identity on comparisons to others, you don't really know who you are. And if you don't know who you are, how can you expect to help your children discover who they are?

How many times have you felt judged? You don't even need to hear judgmental words to know that someone is criticizing you through body language or facial expressions. Even if the other person can hide his or her thoughts, judgment breaks down respect and elevates one person above the other—if only in the mind. As you know, thoughts precede feelings, which precede actions. So, judgment and criticism lead to a breakdown in relationships.

When you begin to feel completely secure in who you are, you will stop judging others. Judgment is simply an indication of someone's insecurity. When you base your identity on comparisons to others, you don't really know who you are. And if you don't know who *you* are, how can you expect to help your children discover who *they* are? If you notice that this is a problem for you, try reviewing principles one and two (connect with your creator and know your true identity).

When I find myself in the company of a judgmental person, I feel like the wall after the excrement hits the fan: contaminated. I generally don't respond because I don't want to give that kind of conversation any momentum.

Take note of how often judgmental statements come out of your own mouth. Sometimes, judging becomes such a habit that we don't even realize we are doing it. As with any bad habit, it takes recognition of the damage you are causing and a concentrated effort to stop and replace it with a more constructive activity.

The Bible cautions us to "first remove the log from your own eye, so you can see clearly to take the speck out of your brother's eye" (Matthew 7:5). It's common to feel irritated by things

> *Try for just one day to pay attention to the judgmental statements that come out of your mouth. Once you are aware of a problem, you can begin to change it.*

in others that you actually struggle with yourself. It's easy to project onto someone else that which we don't like in ourselves but are unwilling to notice.

Certainly, it's normal to observe other people. As a matter of fact, people watching can be a very interesting pastime. It's fun to watch people at the beach or at the mall and try to figure out their stories. However, rather than looking to condemn or judge, just let yourself observe. See them in the light of oneness with their creator. He created them just as he created you. There is a spark of the living God in each one—with potential and promise and creativity. Instead of a judgment, send them a blessing. Change, "Oh my God, look at her hair!" to, "Bless her, Lord, and let her find her fulfillment in you."

Your words either build up or tear down. What you think—and ultimately say—creates your environment. If you wish blessings on others, you open yourself to blessings; if you heap judgment on others, you open yourself to judgment.

When we make judgments, we focus on our differences, often from a negative perspective. We do not approve of the way someone looks or carries himself. We don't like the words he uses or the tone of his voice. We think that person could have presented himself in a different way—a better way—which simply means a way that we would approve. How does that make it right?

When you hear someone behave in a way that you might find obnoxious or rude, it's a good idea to look at yourself, identify how it makes you feel, and then consider whether or not you ever act like that. Use the opportunity to instruct yourself about yourself rather than to judge. Are there any changes that you need to make? Since we are admonished to first take the logs out of our own eyes, this seems to be the only way that we can see clearly to help someone else.

JUDGMENT AND DISCERNMENT ARE TWO DIFFERENT THINGS

According to *Merriam–Webster*, discernment is: the "ability to see and understand people, things, or situations clearly and intelligently." Judgment, on the other hand, as described by the *World English Dictionary*, is: to "assume the position of critic" or to offer "criticism or censure." Each of these uses the powers of observation; one uses those powers to either elevate or put down; the other incorporates all information and decides how it does or doesn't fit into life.

For example, you want to teach children discernment, not fear or judgment. You teach them facts: Cars are big; they go fast; sometimes, the driver can't see a small child. Then, you help them with a plan: Because of these things, we must be cautious when approaching a street and look both ways; cars are not bad; drivers are not bad; but they can still hurt you if you don't stay out of their way.

Kids watch and listen. As a matter of fact, they not only observe you but absorb your energy. If you feel anxious, angry, terrified, or judgmental, they pick that up. You may think they aren't paying attention or that you're hiding your prejudices—wrong.

If you have prejudices or strong feelings, they leak out. Maybe they show through your body language, your eye rolling, your words, or your attitude; the truth is: you cannot hide the energy you emit. It sure would be easier if our energies emitted bright colors, making it obvious to us when others could perceive our red (angry) energy, our green (envious) energy, or our purple (judgmental) energy. Unfortunately, it's not that obvious to you, but it is very clear to your kids—particularly very young children—who absorb everything you send out. They have not yet developed the resources and control to block out negative energy. They don't know they have a choice; and when you don't know you have a choice, you don't.

This is how whole nations (or religions, or political parties, or races) stay divided. The kids harbor the judgments of the parents based on generalization and fear, and they grow up thinking they are right. Why wouldn't they? Everyone they associate with believes a certain way, so they deduce that it must be true. In so doing, we carry our judgments and prejudices and fear from one generation to the other. All prejudice is based on fear. If you feel afraid, you do not emit love; it's just not possible. They are polar opposites, just like: if you look left, you can't also look right. We need to teach our children to rise above these generational judgments and think for themselves. If they feel truly free to love others without the pre-formed opinions and judgments of the community, they can be much more discerning and wise about the choices they make.

Judging others gets in the way. It separates people. It causes factions and divisions which keep you focused on minutiae.

Most of us get so wrapped up in our squabbles that we completely forget the reason we are here on earth. We forget our goals; we lose our direction. We are here to allow God to express himself through us in our own unique way. Who cares if the neighbor drives an SUV? Who cares if the lady at work has "big hair?" Who cares if the boy in your son's class wears an earring? That is really none of your concern.

How does it feel when someone doesn't like the way your child acts or dresses or eats? It feels crummy, doesn't it? You think, "Who do they think they are, judging my kid? They have no right to do that. What business is it of theirs, anyway?"

I think God feels the same way when we criticize or judge one of his kids.

Opinions are not truth; they are just opinions. We need to create an environment in our homes where we see clearly without the clouds of judgment (which are always based on fear of difference). When people are different from us—when they talk differently, dress differently, have different rituals, beliefs, and behaviors—we become suspicious. They are not like us, and we are good. We are cool. We are right. They are different, so they must not be good or cool, or right. Being good, cool, right—those are judgments. Who said? We did. Who are we? One of billions of people on the planet who also think they are good and cool and right. Can billions of people who look different, dress differently, talk different languages, and believe different things all be okay? It's not really our place to say. Certainly, we can discern if we would want to pursue a relationship with them or if it's beneficial to us and our families to act like they act or even if there is a way that we can or should protect ourselves from them. But we don't have to criticize, spew judgment, or make announcements of condemnation. We can feel secure in who we are and understand that everyone is on his or her own journey.

We have to let go of the need to be right and embrace others with the respect that we desire. They have as much right to a choice or a belief or an opinion or a way of dressing as we do. Who made us so sure that we are right?

We make judgments, not having all the information. We mistake our opinions for truth, forgetting that people may see the situation differently. We allow our judgments to divide us, provoke us, and nurture resentments and irritations. How much easier it would be to step back and try to allow things to just be: without labeling them good or bad, lucky or unlucky, or smart or stupid?

If you give others the grace to just be and develop the ability to see the bigger picture, you will reduce your stress levels and stop letting judgments drain your valuable energy. Try it for a day or a week or six months and see how much better you feel. Detach yourself from what slows you down and inhibits God's expression through you.

Let's go to the next peaceful principle: detach. It sounds scary, doesn't it? It's not.

Principle 8:
Detach

"But Jesus did not commit himself to them...for he knew what was in man." —John 2:24–25

"Things arise, and she lets them come; things disappear, and she lets them go.
She has but doesn't possess; acts, but doesn't expect." —Lao Tsu

People often hear me suggest that they detach from a situation and wonder how that is possible. How can I expect them to detach from their kids or their spouse or their job or a traumatic situation?

Detach doesn't mean cease to care. It doesn't mean you become unfeeling or careless. It simply means that you do not allow yourself to get caught up in the drama. It means that you develop a skill of observing and staying clearheaded. It means that rather than rushing into a judgment that comes from panic or anger or fear, you learn to completely center yourself in every situation. Rather than judging, you develop a curiosity about the situation. You look at the bird's-eye view rather than the shortsighted vision that you get when you are too close to a situation. When you respond in anger or fear, you don't think clearly and can make unwise moves, say things you regret, and take unnecessary actions. If you picture a cushion of love between you and the situation, you will make wiser, more authentic decisions. When you get sucked into a situation emotionally, you tend to respond out of your immediate feelings, which you have not necessarily based on truth or wisdom.

> *Detach doesn't mean cease to care. It doesn't mean you become unfeeling or careless. It simply means that you do not allow yourself to get caught up in the drama.*

Imagine for a moment that you are a skilled surgeon. You are the only one on duty in the emergency room. They wheel in a child who has severed his leg in a biking accident. You look at his face, and it is *your child!* Remember, you are the only one who can save this child's leg and possibly his life. What do you do? You take a deep breath and detach—not because you don't love him, but because you do. You realize that your calm demeanor and clear head represent this child's only hope. You cannot react in fear.

That is exactly how you need to parent. Your child depends on you to know what you are doing and to know what is best. If you continually get caught up in the emotion of the moment, if you take every confrontation personally, if you constantly feel offended or hurt or angry, you will never be an effective parent. If you fear what people will say and fear that your child is headed for disaster, you will react rather than act. Reaction is never the best response unless you are in a burning building and need to grab your kids and run (or some similar emergency). The rest of the time, it is important to stay calm and curious.

Ask yourself questions about what might make your child act a certain way or what he or she might be trying to say but doesn't

> Taking a deep breath first means you have less to clean up later.

have the vocabulary to express. How might he or she feel? What's really going on? Never assume that your child is trying to destroy you. Assume that he or she has a need, and that you have the answer. You cannot accurately assess any need unless you detach and look at the situation from the perspective of: "How can I help? What is best in this situation?" If you react out of anger or fear, you might just strike out by yelling or smacking and demanding that the behavior stop immediately. Almost everyone has done this from time to time. The truth is: you get the behavior to stop. However, you still don't know what caused it, and you have just chased your child into his or her shell to retreat from you because you are not safe. You have also taught your child that yelling and hitting are effective communication tools—great.

If you stop and take a deep breath before you respond and communicate your desires clearly—as shown in the next principle—you will find that you have less to clean up later.

Principle 9:
Communicate Clearly

"Learn to listen as though every word you hear were the oxygen you needed to breathe."—Jill Kamp Melton, The Power of the Zip
"The first duty of love is to listen." —Paul Tillich

We could head off so many difficult situations at the pass by simply learning to communicate effectively. In my experience, most miscommunication stems from one of four causes: making assumptions; reacting from emotion instead of fact; not hearing what is really being said; or bringing in past history, thereby clouding the immediate issue at hand.

> *In my experience, most miscommunication stems from one of four causes: making assumptions; reacting from emotion instead of fact; not hearing what is really being said; or bringing in past history, thereby clouding the immediate issue at hand.*

With this in mind, here are five points to remember for enhancing your communication skills:

1. Never make any assumptions.

2. Take a deep breath and calm down before communicating.

3. Listen attentively without previewing in your mind how you will defend yourself.

4. Speak about the issue at hand clearly, without dragging in past issues.

5. Clarify.

Communication breaks down in a relationship when we think we know the other party so well that we assume we know how he or she will respond. In this case, we feel justified jumping right in with anger or exasperation because, "You should have known!" or, "I've told you this a hundred times!" Often one partner will assume he or she knows the facts without asking. If one partner comes home late from work, the other assumes the late one was being thoughtless by not calling. The same goes with your children. Because we tend to base all assumptions on past behaviors, we sometimes don't give them credit for the changes they do make. So from the beginning of the communication, the stage has been set with emotions already lit.

Five points to enhance communication

1. *Never make any assumptions.*

2. *Take a deep breath and calm down before communicating.*

3. *Listen attentively without previewing in your mind how you will defend yourself.*

4. *Speak about the issue at hand clearly, without dragging in past issues.*

5. *Clarify.*

This is why it's important to take a deep breath and allow yourself to calm down and shake off any preconceived notions before you begin. When you have no agenda and are not clouded by emotion, you can look into your child's eyes and listen attentively—with no need to prepare for a defense while he or she is speaking and no need to go on the attack. You have no reason to be defensive, so you can clearly hear what is being said. If you are not poised to hurl an accusation, you can state how you feel clearly, and you can curiously learn about the situation. Without making any assumptions about his or her intention, you can state what you want to say and be prepared to hear the answer.

Because we often misunderstand or misspeak, it makes sense to clarify by asking what your child means or restating what you think you heard and giving him or her a chance to clarify. Always validate the emotion you hear. People respond better when they feel heard and understood. Stephen Covey says, "Seek first to understand; then, to be understood." If we just followed this one principle in communication, we would save ourselves a lot of heartache. Instead, most of us—when we should be listening—prepare our defense. We feel the need to be right, and that automatically makes the other person wrong. So, someone walks away feeling unheard, invalidated, and probably ticked off.

I have people come into my office swearing they will do anything to fix the marriage or the parent-child relationship. Unfortunately, when it comes right down to it, that means they'll do anything *except* give up the need to be right. If there are winners and losers in an argument or interaction, tension will remain in the home. No one wants to be the loser. No one wants to be wrong. So let's look at ways to create win/win situations.

> The need to be right may be killing your relationships!

Certainly, you can't let your three-year-old run out in the street. There's no way you would want your four-teen-year-old to go to a party without any parents home. You probably don't want your child to exist on a diet of donuts and soda pop. So, there are times when you will have to deny your kids what they want. But that doesn't mean they have to walk away feeling like losers or that you have not heard or understood or respected them. We all have areas in which we can grow and learn, so we have to open ourselves to growing and learning. Be curious in your conversations with your child. Ask questions that will get to the heart of what they really want. "So, who's going to be at the party that you are eager to see?" Validate their feelings. "Yes, a donut sure would taste good right now." Show them you understand. "It feels so good to just run freely, doesn't it?" And then help each child to find a way to get that desire met in a way that makes you feel comfortable.

Ask when your son would like to have that particular friend over or maybe go to a movie together. Suggest that your daughter select a great treat after eating a healthy dinner. Affirm the need to run, but give an alternative place to run free, showing the difference between safe places to run and places where you need to exert more wisdom.

I hear parents say all the time that it's important for their kids to learn a healthy fear about things like cars, strangers, or unsupervised parties. I disagree. I don't think it's ever necessary to instill fear in a child. I do, however, think it's important to teach children wisdom and discernment. Love and fear are polar opposites. Love is expressed in a life in which someone feels secure and confident. In such a life, there is nothing to fear. But you still don't want to run in the street. You want to have enough knowledge about speeding cars and how they can hurt you coupled with the wisdom to not put yourself in that position. The point is not to teach your kids to be afraid of cars or traffic. You just don't want them to go running out in the middle of it!

A couple of things happen when you feel fearful—just like when you feel angry. Your body goes into fight-or-flight mode, secreting adrenalin, making your heart beat faster, and rushing your blood to your extremities so you can fight or flee. But when your blood rushes to your arms and legs, it is *not* rushing to your brain. So while your arms and legs might work well, your brain is not functioning at full capacity. Therefore, when you teach your kids to be afraid, you're teaching them to be stupid, which, according to the dictionary, means, "proceeding from mental dullness." I don't presume to tell you what you want, but I, for one, want wise kids—not stupid kids.

And this is true of you as well. It is far more advantageous *not* to respond out of fear or anger or while in full fight-or-flight mode but to always communicate from a place of calm, clear wisdom. Take a breath...then speak.

No matter what offense has taken place or what amount of invalidation or disobedience, it is important not only for the sake of the relationship but for your own health to forgive and to forgive quickly—as you will learn in the next chapter.

SECRET 10:
FORGIVE QUICKLY

"The weak can never forgive. Forgiveness is the attribute of the strong."
—*Mahatma Gandhi*

So often, people have trouble with forgiveness because of what they think it means. They think it means excusing bad behavior. They think if they forgive, things will continue the way they have been, and the other person won't change his or her behavior. They think it means being weak or not standing up for what is right. They feel they are right and deserve to be angry and hold onto resentment or a grudge.

Forgiveness never says hurtful behavior is okay. It doesn't mean that you can't still press charges or ask for an apology or restitution. It doesn't mean that you must

> It has been said that unforgiveness is like drinking poison and expecting the other person to die.

stay trapped in an unhealthy relationship. And it has nothing to do with who is right or wrong. Yes, you have every right to your feelings; however, hanging onto bitterness and the need for revenge because you have that right doesn't make any sense because you're the one whose stomach is in knots. You're the one getting headaches from the stress. You're the one refusing to trust anyone ever again, creating your own prison of loneliness because someone hurt you.

You must choose to release the offense if you want to be free. You get more of what you put out there. If you put unforgiveness out into the world, the negative consequences come back to you. If you don't forgive, then you punish yourself for a wrong done by someone else. I believe that is partly what Jesus meant in Matthew 6 when he said, "But if you do not forgive men their sins, your Father will not forgive your sins." Once you have forgiven someone, it takes the responsibility for revenge out of your hands. God says he will take care of it. He knows that it will destroy you if you cannot let it go. It's like holding onto old dynamite: you never know when it's going to explode.

This is the final principle in my list, but it is by no means least. As Marianne Williamson, spiritual teacher and author of *Return to Love* said, "The practice of forgiveness is our most important contribution to the healing of the world." Without it, we are unable to move on—unable to heal. We get stuck in a rut of pain that begins to feel as familiar as an old shoe, and no matter how that old shoe is destroying our walk, we refuse to give it up. We have whole cultures that cannot move on because someone has not apologized or made amends.

The problem here is that if the person who owes you an apology dies without making amends and you have given that person the key to your happiness and joy, you have totally given up your ability to feel joy again. Not only is that totally unnecessary but it's so foolish. You must never give away control of your own attitude by blaming someone else. Yes, they may be guilty, but you should never give them the power to control you with that. As a matter of fact, they probably don't even know you've given them control. Chances are, they have moved on with their lives, and here you sit with an ulcer festering in your gut. How could that ever make sense?

> "The practice of forgiveness is our most important contribution to the healing of the world." —Marianne Williamson

Choosing not to forgive friends is bad. And choosing not to forgive family—particularly your own children—is worse. I've worked with dozens of parents of adult children willing—even eager —to cut their kids off for some perceived slight. The son doesn't call frequently enough. The daughter missed a family reunion for one reason or another. I'll tell you what I tell them: If you don't want a relationship with your kids, bravo. You're on your way to accomplishing just that. But if you do, you have to allow them to be human, to have their own lives, and to make decisions you sometimes disagree with. The more you manipulate with your unwillingness to forgive, the further you push your kids away.

And it doesn't matter how old your children are. If you hang on to anger, hatred, irritation, hurt, offense, or similar emotions, refusing to forgive and let it go, you are pushing your kids away. The truth is you have much more power and influence over your children if you learn to release any wrong and reinforce your love for them. As soon as they feel like you have cut off your love for them, whether you have or not, you have begun to drive them away. When you drive them away, they will seek wisdom and affirmation elsewhere: maybe through their peers, another adult, or, God forbid, someone who will promise them the world and destroy their lives with drugs or prostitution or abuse. All this can be prevented by making forgiveness a regular practice. Certainly, making restitution for wrongs, delivering apologies, and talking things through are also important. But you will never get the chance if you withhold your love by clinging tenaciously to unforgiveness.

So, in fact, we are talking about your freedom here. Your freedom is in your hands. You are only responsible for you. Constantly reminding someone of what they have done is counterproductive in a relationship. Resolve things as best you can and move on. Will you choose to be free and peaceful? It's up to you.

PART THREE:
REAL LIFE

How Do I Get My Kids to Obey Me?

"Children, always obey your parents, for this pleases the Lord."
—Colossians 3:20

As a kid and as a young parent, it seemed to me as if a parent's main goal was to get children to obey—period. Many of us were raised by the old conventional wisdom that children should be seen and not heard. So, we figured it was right. We all know homes in which parents used statements like: "Wait until your father gets home," and "I'm the mommy, that's why!" as well as actions like yelling, grounding, and spanking. Maybe you grew up in a house like that. Maybe it sounds a bit like your house now.

Maybe there was or is a lot of tension in your home. If you grew up in this environment—even if you found it harsh, even if you felt insignificant, even if it made you angry, even if you swore you would never do those things—chances are, you'll find the same patterns repeating themselves in your own home. Why? Because as a very young child, you developed your reasoning skills, your verbal skills, your sense of who you are, and your place in the world in that environment. You learned right from wrong. You learned what is acceptable and what is not. By the time you turned six, you pretty much had all that figured out. Can it be changed? Yes. But typically, we don't change it because we believe we're right. And why not? Our parents, whom we looked to as God, taught us these things, and they would never lead us astray: not in a million years—unthinkable.

Well, the fact is, your parents learned their world view (which includes parenting techniques) from their moms and dads. And their moms and dads learned from their parents before them. And so it continues. We store in our subconscious exactly that: a whole lot of unconscious thoughts we believe are right because our parents said so. Now that you are a grown-up and understand that everyone is a product of his or her environment and that everyone has a particular DNA and is born with a bent toward a particular kind of personality, you have the cognitive abilities to look at this in a slightly more analytical manner and to ask questions. But many of us—most of us—don't. We just keep acting the same way and hope things get better. Didn't Albert Einstein say that the definition of insanity is doing the same things over and over again and expecting different results? Indeed, he did.

"Well, I turned out fine," you reason. Did you? Is it "fine" with you to worry all the time? Is it "fine" with you to have conflicts with your kids over and over again? Is it "fine" with you when your kid is out of control, and you scream at him or her because it's the only thing you can think to do? I remember when my son was about eight: I was getting ready to give him a spanking—I don't even recall why at this point—and he looked up at me and said, "I thought you didn't believe in spanking anymore!" In all my motherly wisdom, I answered, "I don't! I just don't know what else to do." How's that for an honest assessment of the situation? Now I know there are better options, but at the time I just couldn't see them. That's why I wrote this book: to help you be aware of healthier, more effective options.

Even as I tried to figure it out, every parenting book I could get my hands on still maintained obedience as the goal. Even my pastor held this opinion. So, every time my kids spun out of control or wouldn't sit and be quiet or obey every command, I assumed I was failing at the task of parenting and had to crank it up a notch.

Holding my fifteen-month-old daughter, I had a conversation with that pastor. My daughter, of course, was not as interested in the conversation as I was, and she started wriggling to get down. She squirmed and leaned over my arms so that I had a hard time focusing. The pastor looked at me and said, "She needs to be spanked!" Really? Maybe I wasn't handling her very gracefully, but I was smart enough to know that fifteen-month-old babies run around and explore—it's their job. It's not their job to have an in-depth conversation with a pastor after holding it together, being good in the nursery. My daughter needed to run around. I just needed to take the time to affirm that need, to let her know that I heard her and that she would get a chance in a second, to tell the pastor that we would resume our conversation at a better time, and to walk away. Once again, I felt like a bad parent because someone whom I assumed knew more than I expressed his opinion. So I walked away with self-doubt but no helpful information. I just knew his response didn't make sense to me.

According to the "children are to be seen and not heard" wisdom, the goal was to get her to stop squirming and shut up. And again, maybe I could have made her shut up. But the point is, while obedience and respect for parents talking is important, another step needs to happen first. It takes more thought. It takes more time; but in the long run, you raise a child who doesn't just shut down but respects you and wants to please you.

So what's the magic bullet? What is this great wisdom? It's a relationship. It's not the kind of magic bullet that you shoot out of a gun and pierce into the heart of the matter: it's a magic bullet that you make yourself. In Bob Goff's heart-warming book, *Love Does*, he tells the story of how his dad used to make his own ammunition. "The polished brass shell casings might as well have been gold coins in his hand, and my dad would sit in a chair by the window, filling the casings with gunpowder he pulled from a small bag at his feet." I can picture his dad sitting there with Bob (as a little boy, watching him take such care), really enjoying the process of creating something. Sure, his dad could have gone the traditional route and bought bullets for his guns, but instead, he blazed his own path. He loved the engagement, the close proximity, the hands-on approach, and the feeling of doing something that made a difference to him.

So sure, we could get our kids to obey us the old, conventional way by expecting results and not worrying about the process. Or we can create our own magic bullet. It takes more time. It involves a hands-on approach and an investment of thought and care. But we'll produce a better product—one that more accurately reaches the goal: a secure, well-adjusted human being who likes to spend time with you and wants to do what you say not because he or she fears you or wants to avoid the confusion and pain of your anger and displeasure, but because your child trusts you.

Building a relationship with your child is different from being his best buddy. You are still his parent, and for his safety and well-being, he does need to learn to obey. But rather than making that the ultimate goal, make it a by-product of a close, trusting, and respectful relationship.

You will not accomplish this by being louder, bigger, stronger, or more powerful. You will accomplish it by thinking things through—no matter what the "authorities" say. You will accomplish it by joining your child where he is and producing change from there.

Jay Morgan, author of a great book about conscious parenting, *Fingerpainting in Psych Class*, tells a powerful story of Milton Erickson.

Dr. Erickson was a student at an inpatient facility for the mentally ill. There was a particularly difficult patient there who was delusional: he thought he was Jesus Christ.... No amount of confrontation, reality testing, medication, or therapy could convince him otherwise and help him break through the delusion....

Dr. Erickson asked the more veteran staff if he could take a run at him. The staff agreed. Dr. Erickson found the patient and walked with him, talking casually, until they got to the arts and crafts room. Dr. Erickson then addressed the patient, simply saying, "I understand you do some carpentry work." The patient did not argue or protest. Dr. Erickson and the patient then began a woodworking project... all the while talking and getting to know each other better....

This illustrates an important approach Dr. Erickson termed, "joining the patient." Dr. Erickson formulated an approach where the patient could offer him no resistance. (Jesus was a carpenter; therefore, the patient had to be a carpenter if he wanted to maintain his delusion.) Dr. Erickson then joined the patient, built a therapeutic relationship, and led him out of his delusional state.

As a parent, you will sometimes have to insist a child join you to get ready for school on time, join you to complete their homework, or join you to help clean the dishes. But don't forget to join them too. It will help you to understand your children and guide you to novel and effective ways to help them.

Always be conscious of surrounding your child with a cushion of love. Take a deep breath and think before you respond. Is there a way you can join your child and lead him or her where you want that child to go?

WHAT DO I DO WHEN MY KIDS GET ANGRY?

"In your anger, do not sin: Do not let the sun go down while you are still angry." —*Ephesians 4:6*
"My four-year-old got so angry at his brother that he took the TV remote and threw it, shattering our $1,500 television! What am I to do?" —*Frustrated Mom*

So, what makes a kid so mad? Well, lots of things. What makes you mad? Remember: kids are simply small people. They have the same feelings we do. They just don't have the cognitive skills or emotional resources that an adult has to deal with them. (I'm not saying we all use those resources, but at least we have them at our disposal.)

Because they don't have the resources and discernment to express emotions

> Loneliness, fear, embarrassment, anxiety, hurt, physical discomfort, and powerlessness all masquerade as anger.

in a clear, succinct way, they often act out. Anger serves as a catchall emotion for kids. Loneliness, fear, embarrassment, anxiety, hurt, physical discomfort, and powerlessness all masquerade as anger.

Now, let's be clear: aggression is different from anger. Anger is an emotion, and emotions are never bad. They are just information; when you have the information that something made you angry, you can then decide to do something about it. Aggression, on the other hand, is a behavior or disposition that hurts or intimidates someone else or infringes on someone else's rights, threatening or causing harm. One is acceptable; the other is not. You need to teach your child the difference.

First, you must teach him how to de-escalate. Have him take a deep breath (or two or three); it might help to look him in the eye and do it with him. "Okay, Tommy, breathe in and blow it out. Do it again. Do you feel your body calming down? In... out. In...out." This little exercise will help you refrain from flying off the handle too. When he calms down, move on.

Next, help him identify his true feelings (whether anger or embarrassment or fear) and name the emotion. Then, help him identify what caused it—ask him. You might have to suggest some options because he may not have the words. For example:

He says: "Jimmy was making fun of me!"

You suggest: "You felt embarrassed because your brother made fun of you in front of his friends."

Or he says: "Sandy won't give me my turn!"

And you suggest: "You felt powerless because you didn't know how to get your sister to give you your turn playing with the video game."

Help him brainstorm actions that might have been more effective. Feel free to give suggestions.

"Use your words and tell someone how you feel."

Or, "You could have played something else for a while and then taken a nice long turn when your sister and her friend were done."

Encourage him to come up with his own alternatives so he feels more empowered and can feel the responsibility of controlling his actions next time.

Certainly, it's important to share your true feelings—in a calm and straightforward way. Remember: more is caught than taught, and if you scream and yell and overreact or over-value the TV more than your child, you teach him something different from what you want to teach him. Try something like: "I feel really sad and angry that you broke the new TV. I worked very hard to make the money to buy that, and it hurts that you didn't think of that before you threw the remote. Let's try to figure out a way that it doesn't happen again."

Then, of course, you need to have some sort of discussion about: "What do we do now?" You have a broken TV that will have to be replaced. Since you worked hard to make the money in the first place, maybe you could have your child brainstorm fair consequences with you. Of course, a kid will have a little trouble coming up with $1,500. But he could do some chores around the house and put the money he earns into a "replace-the-TV" money jar. Remember, the fact that the TV cost you $1,500 should not be the issue. I know that's financially painful to you, but the consequence should not be so extreme because of the value. Your child is four and doesn't know $1,500 from fifteen cents. The consequence should be the same if your child broke a lamp or a glass. The problem to be addressed is really the anger and how to deal with it in a healthy, constructive way rather than through aggression.

> The most important thing you can do to ensure your child exhibits healthy behaviors is to model healthy behaviors.

Remember, your child needs direction. He needs to know how *not* to react like that. He doesn't need you to inflate the situation by getting out of control yourself. It's your job to teach your child how to do better next time. And your child needs to know you still love him. Give him a hug and get him to help you sweep up the mess. Your child needs to know that he can control his emotions, even when they are strong. Your child needs assurance that big emotions don't scare you. And he needs to learn new ways to express those strong feelings. Your child can be part of solution and still know he is loved.

Creating an atmosphere in your home that lessens the chance of those kinds of things happening is a good preventative measure.

1. Catch your child responding well when you notice he didn't throw something when he could have.

2. Compliment your child when he is not slamming, hitting, or yelling.

3. Refrain from verbally monitoring your child constantly so he doesn't carry extra tension.

4. Encourage regular physical activity: both organized and free play.

5. Show interest in your child and what he is doing so he feels valued.

6. Maintain a sense of humor whenever you can. Everything doesn't have to be so dark and serious.

7. And don't forget to address with big sister or big brother the issue that caused the uproar in the first place. Everyone needs to accept his or her share of responsibility in the ordeal.

The most important thing you can do to ensure your child exhibits healthy behaviors is to model healthy behaviors. Make it a common practice to develop in your own life the principles of peaceful parenting from the previous chapters. The goal is not to control your children but to help them develop self-control. The goal isn't even to get your child to obey or act appropriately. The goal is to raise happy, healthy, secure kids who want to be with you and want to listen to you because they feel secure in your relationship and don't want to disappoint you; then, you will meet those smaller goals along the way.

How Can I Get Some Cooperation Around the House?

"My kids never help around the house. I do everything *for* everyone *and I am tired of it. I never get any time for myself!"*
—*Mom complaint*

Recognizing the problem is the first step toward change. You won't help anyone in the long run if you are running ragged, unhappy, and angry. So when you feel that way, it's an indication that the time has come to make changes.

Are you the type of parent who feels like it's just easier if you do everything yourself? Do you feel this way because nobody else does it right, and you feel like you have to do it over again anyway? Or is it because you get tired of reminding or asking? Does it make you feel needed?

You must identify why things are the way they are, or the situation will not change. If you have a strong "why," you can probably draw on the resources within you to make a change happen.

> Recognizing the problem is the first step toward change.

If you do all the household chores yourself because no one else does them correctly, perhaps it would help to show your children how to do the chores the way you think is best; or perhaps you need to relax your standards a bit. This is also part of building that ever-important relationship. Cleaning with Mom can be fun! Putting toys away with Dad can become a game full of laughs and giggles.

Keep in mind that it is your job to train your kids to do things properly—all the while modeling the kind of attitude that you expect from them. If they grow up thinking chores are fun, you won't have any trouble getting them to help out. If you expect them to help out, the kids will get used to it. On the other hand, if you issue random commands when you are in a bad mood or have tripped over that toy truck one too many times so that you scream for them to get this room picked up, *now*, the whole event will take on a different color.

If you find yourself nagging, make a rule that encourages your children to:

1. Do chores without a reminder. When you have an inanimate object to consult (like a chart), you can always say, "What does the chart say that you have to do before you go outside?" That takes the pressure

off of *your* relationship and puts the onus on a piece of paper.

2.   Do things the first time they are asked. Be respectful of them and agree on a time that works for both of you. Again, if you have a chart, you can specify the time frame that way.

When kids know that it's a household rule to set the table before they watch TV or they understand that a snack and then homework is the order of the day every day, then they understand that's just the way it is. Give them something to look forward to after they finish: playing outside, having one-on-one time with you, taking a bike ride, watching a movie, or doing whatever motivates them.

If you do all the household chores yourself because it makes you feel needed, it's important to find some outside activities that give you pleasure and that use your gifts and talents. Self-nurturing is vital for maintaining your energy, self-respect, and sense of well-being. It also sets an important precedent for your kids. It shows them that you respect yourself and will encourage them to also respect you. (You can read more about this in the "Respect" section in Part II.)

If, in fact, you have never expected your kids to assume certain responsibilities or have never taught them to take any on, now is the time. Children need to be assigned clear responsibilities for a couple of reasons: first, it helps your kids feel like a necessary part of the family unit, and second, fulfilling responsibilities builds a sense of self-esteem and accomplishment. Give little ones a mop or toilet brush or scrub brush of their own so that they can work alongside you. It becomes something fun to do with Mommy. As they get older, they can be trusted with more chores under supervision—and then alone.

> If you have never expected your kids to assume certain responsibilities or have never taught them to take any on, now is the time.

Tasks and responsibilities must be age appropriate. Most kids can learn pretty early to separate different colors for the wash. Later, they can learn to operate the washer and dryer. Maybe they can take responsibility for washing and putting away their own clothes, or they can learn to fold towels.

Tackling chores a little at a time and doing things together are good ways to start. See what tasks they enjoy, observe what they do well, and mention it to them. You could even give them kudos at the dinner table in front of the whole family. Different children will gravitate toward different chores. Some will prefer doing the dishes or setting the table or vacuuming. Give them a choice so they feel like they have input.

MODEL GRATITUDE

Model gratitude by thanking your children when they help with the workload. Tell them how their behavior affects you: "Wow, that really takes a load off Mommy." "Thanks, that gives us time to go to the park." "When your room is neat, I am more inclined to let you have your friends over to play."

Your children will feel better when they have a less stressed mom, so it works better for everyone. Just breathe and release some of your perfectionist tendencies. You'll feel better too.

How Do I Handle a Negative Child?

"My eight-year-old stepdaughter is forever pouting like a 'sad sack.' She's always looking for someone to feel sorry for her and forever comparing what she has to how much others have and coming up short. It's so annoying that sometimes I feel like screaming, 'Get a life!' I don't like to be around her, yet my husband and I have her every other weekend. She throws the whole family off kilter."
—Irritated Stepmom

When a child develops a "victim mentality," it can be very annoying; but more importantly, very dangerous. Not only will you find it unpleasant to be around the constant negativity, but a child with a victim mentality can fall victim to predators who have a special radar for that sort of thing. So it is very important to help her build up her sense of well-being.

While using words like "forever" and "always" might seem accurate in the quote above, I would encourage you to look for times when this is not the case—when she is pleasant and fun to be around—then begin to focus on those. Comment on those. Catch her being positive and generous.

Having the ability to throw the whole household out of whack is an awful lot of power for a child. It may be the only way that she feels she has any control or gets any attention. She is a child, and she has limited resources compared to the adults in her life, so let's work on getting some balance here. The adults should set the tone in the home—not the kids. Kids feel more secure when they know that they are not responsible for everyone else's feelings—even if it appears that they enjoy "making everyone crazy." So, let's examine some ways that you can regain control.

Present your observations to your spouse in a nonjudgmental way. He is likely to be sensitive to any accusations about his daughter. Explain the dangers that threaten the unity of your family but also the dangers that threaten her well-being. Maybe both of you—together with your stepdaughter's birth mother—can agree on what to say and how to respond when she behaves this way. If you don't have a good relationship with the birth mom, that's okay. You can choose to work something out with your husband and your stepdaughter's mom or work out your own solution and response.

Your stepdaughter needs you. Here are ten tips that might help.

1. Change the way you see the child. She is an innocent girl who has had difficult situations in her life. She feels misunderstood and unimportant and lonely. Detach from whatever resentments and irritations you might have around her, your husband, or her mom.

2. Understand that she is in your life for a reason—maybe to help you grow—but more importantly, she needs what *you* have to offer.

3. Spend time with her: particularly during those times between pouting sessions when she seems more open. Help her discover her unique talents and skills and interests.

4. Encourage her to grow in these areas of strength and interest. Take family outings around activities that encourage these things.

5. Give her responsibilities at your house so she doesn't feel like an outsider and follow through with making sure they are done. She needs to be treated and feel as if she is a part of your family. She must abide by the rules of your home, and I would encourage you to lovingly enforce the rules.

6. Expect her to succeed and verbalize that expectation to her.

7. Encourage her to dream; help her develop a plan to achieve those dreams. Sometimes, kids just need to know that they are important enough to be heard.

8. Teach her, by words and example, the power of gratitude.

9. Give her loving eye contact and tell her plainly and firmly that you care too much to allow self-pity or negative behavior. Do not reinforce her self-pity in any way: either by giving into it or being disgusted or irritated by it. Any validation (positive or negative) will reinforce it.

10. Do not get sucked into drama or gossip about her mother or allow her to put a wedge between you and her father. Keep communication open and make sure you and your husband do not hide things from each other. Stay united. Keep talking—and breathe.

As always, she is learning from you. You may only have a stepchild for limited amounts of time, but in those moments, with focused attention, she can begin to regain her power and her self-esteem. When she knows her true identity and is secure in your love, she will no longer need the negative focus to get attention. Remember that she needs your example, so it is important for you to practice the principles of peaceful parenting in your life. Where there is real, unconditional love, there is no fear. They cannot exist together.

What's the Best Way to Deal with Sibling Rivalry?

"And while they were in the field, Cain attacked his brother, Abel, and killed him." —Genesis 3:8

A certain amount of competition and irritation are normal among kids. However, it's important to teach children certain life skills, such as: respect, emotional control, and healthy conflict resolution. What better place to teach these skills than in the home, where the tests are the greatest—as are the rewards.

> Teach your kids that there are no unacceptable feelings—just unacceptable behaviors.

Here are a few tips that may help you:

Teach your kids that there are no unacceptable feelings—just unacceptable behaviors. When their arguments start to escalate, show them some physical ways that they can safely release their anger, frustration, etc. For example:

- They can run to release their feelings.

- They can draw pictures.

- They can jump on a trampoline.

- They can write about their feelings.

- They can scream into a pillow or pound a pillow.

Children, like adults, need to learn to identify their feelings and then communicate those feelings appropriately. So, do not shut them down but offer them acceptable alternatives for expressing their feelings.

After your children have calmed down, encourage them to look at their siblings face-to-face to apologize and talk it out if necessary. You can model good eye contact. It is very validating.

Help them identify the problem. "Davey won't share his water pistol with me." Then help them talk through a solution. Help them put words to it. "Susan wants to play with the water pistol; Davey's playing with it now. Davey, when will you be through playing with your water pistol so Susan can have a turn? Susan, what can you do in the meantime until he's finished?"

Make the absolute rules and consequences very clear. (For example, physical violence is *never* acceptable or allowed.)

Don't make *too* many rules but rules that really count and that, if broken, will trigger real and unpleasant consequences and enforcement on your part.

Offer positive experiences as a reward if they get through the rest of the day without screaming at each other: consider a family bike ride, a trip to the park, or an outing for ice cream to encourage positive family experiences as something to anticipate with joy.

Make sure you model these healthy behaviors yourself so that you practice what you preach, because all in all, *more behavior is caught than taught.* And of course, *just breathe.*

How Can I Stop My Child's Tantrums?

"My three-year-old has tantrums that make him so out of control that he just screams at me. I try to give him time-outs, but that just escalates things. I don't know what to do! Do you have any suggestions?" —Another Frustrated Mom

Kids do not have the inner resources to process strong negative emotions, and we adults often don't either. So, we end up teaching them to knock it off and swallow their feelings, leaving the adrenaline and other stress hormones circulating in their bodies with no place to go. A lifetime of swallowing and suppressing your feelings can play havoc with your immune system. We need to teach our kids to acknowledge their strong negative emotions—such as anger, frustration, and sadness—and then physically release those feelings.

I read once that ducks can glide along peacefully in a pond, come into each other's territory, and get into a little battle.

As they swim away from each other after the battle is over, they each flap their wings a few times and then continue to glide peacefully. If only humans could deal with conflict so effectively.

Recently, my grandson had a bit of a fit himself (because he wasn't getting his way), and then he started pouting. I told him the story of the ducks and asked him if he could flap his wings and do an anger dance to get the anger out of his body. Reluctantly at first, he started to flap his wings and wiggle around. As he did this, he started to laugh, which released negative feelings. The issue was quickly resolved. Later in the day, a similar thing happened, and I said, "Did you forget to do your anger dance?" He started smiling, flapped his arms a bit, and that was that.

It can be embarrassing when your kid has an all-out melt-down in the grocery store. Sometimes, the judgmental stares that other frustrated shoppers send your way can feel pretty intimidating. Remember principle four: breathe. Other people's opinions are just that: opinions. They are based on their own experiences, and I would venture to say they all forget when their own children had meltdowns in the supermarket.

Just stay focused on your goal. Remember, your child is frustrated and too young to verbalize what is going on in his mind. So it's your job to help him. It's fine if you want to pick your child up and remove him from the store out of respect for the other shoppers but do so gently, firmly telling him that you will talk it out in the car. If you want to work it out in the store, go ahead. Just keep your voice calm and steady. Tell your child to breathe in and breathe out. Allow him time to calm down. You can breathe along with him.

Once the child is calm, affirm what is going on and validate him. "You're angry because Mommy won't let you have that candy. I know that's frustrating, and you're probably hungry too. It would be fun to have all the candy in the store, but we can't do that right now." Help him figure out a way to meet his needs then help him anticipate meeting that need as soon as possible. "Why don't we plan a great snack that we can have as soon as we get home. Then, let's cooperate as much as we can so we can get home quickly to your snack."

> Remember, your child is frustrated and too young to verbalize what is going on in his mind. So it's your job to help him.

When you get home where things aren't as hectic and you don't have an audience, you can ask him to think about a better way to let you know that he is mad. Can your child use his words? Can he make a drawing? Ask your child how he might get rid of all that frustration physically. Maybe he could jump around when he gets out of the store. You can calmly explain that there are places where it's not okay to make noise and jump around, but that he can always do it outside.

Remember that it's a child's job to push the envelope. Children will always look for the boundaries and will always need an affirmation of your love. Try not to react in anger and embarrassment when they are just doing their job. It's your job to show them where the boundaries are and teach them to express themselves in an acceptable manner. There's no reason to lose your cool over that. It's just what kids and mommies do.

So, teach your kids to acknowledge their feelings and name them. Don't make it a sin to feel negative emotions. No emotion is wrong or a sin, but there are healthy and unhealthy ways to express emotions and deal with them. One of those unhealthy ways is to stuff them. A creative and healthy way is to create an anger dance or frustration dance to let the bad feelings out of the body. Learn to talk about the emotion and release it. Then, it can be truly gone. If your kids learn to stuff it, the emotion is never really gone, will squeak out at the most unsuspected times, and may harm their health by compromising their immune systems. So, it really is healthier to address it.

Don't let other people's opinions determine how you will parent. Your child is your most important focus—not the opinions of others.

What Do I Do When My Child Is Defiant?

"He was a silent fury who no torment could tame."
—Jack London, White Fang
"You must carry a chaos within you to give birth to a dancing star."
—Nietzsche

If we start with the premise that we should be able to control our children, we head down a slippery path. We have children not to control them but to guide and nurture them.

Any parent knows that you cannot *make* a teenager do anything. Small children are at a disadvantage, physically. You can physically control them because you are bigger and stronger and often because they fear punishment. If you practice this parenting strategy, you are in for a rude awakening when your child turns the tables on you and becomes too big for you to physically control—and it doesn't take long for them to get there.

How does it feel for you when others try to control you? You feel angry and resistant; you want to do what you want to do, and because you can't, you feel frustrated. You try to explain how you feel, but they don't care, so you feel negated and invalidated. When someone, perhaps a boss or a spouse, tries to exert too much control over you, you probably begin to resemble a wet noodle that can't be pushed around. No one can really *make* you do anything. If you end up complying, it's certainly not because you want to. It's because you figure you have to in order to get something you want—like a paycheck. But your morale plummets; you feel less than enthusiastic, and the first chance you get, you will do whatever you darn well please. You bear no warm, fuzzy thoughts toward the controlling person, do you?

If you agree, then you already understand exactly how your child feels.

What would make a difference in the way you feel toward your boss or spouse? Would it help if, instead of commanding you to write a report now, she asked if you were available to write that report immediately—or, if not, when might you be available to do it? Now, it feels like you have some wiggle room; you have a choice. Yes, you still have to write the report—maybe even sometime today—but you can choose when to do it. Okay, that's fair. You might not be thrilled with it, but you understand that this is what work is all about.

Would it make a difference if you had a warm, friendly relationship with your boss? Would it help to know he or she cared about your family and your sick mother and really empathized with the limited amount of time you have to get things done? Would it help if you had some fun times with your boss too—with no work pressure: just enjoying each other's company? It's always easier to respond favorably to someone who likes you, who enjoys being with you, and who "gets" you.

Why do we expect that it's any different for our kids?

When a child digs his or her heels in, the child uses his or her personal power the only way he or she knows how. If

> A struggle over wills is a lose/lose proposition.

you have ever known someone with an eating disorder, you know how this feels. You can plead and beg and bribe and punish, but as long as you think it's about food, you are missing the mark. It's about control: about combating feelings of helplessness and inadequacy. The only thing the person feels he or she can control is his or her food intake. And he or she will die trying to prove that unless you can get to the underlying issues and needs.

So, when your child acts defiantly and you continue to try to control what you can never control, the child wins. But, of course, he or she loses in the long run, and so do you. A struggle over wills is a lose/lose proposition. You have to figure out what your child needs. He or she is not just trying to ruin your day or prove that you are in idiot. The child is, however, trying to make some point that is probably lost on you at the moment. Go back to the peaceful parenting principles again and practice detaching. Let go of your need to be right for the moment and see if you can step back and determine what's really going on.

Probably at least 80 percent of the time, you can resolve the issue by creating a closer, more respectful relationship with your child. His or her emotional needs are just like yours. First and foremost, each of us wants to feel loved. If you think that going to work and bringing home the money should make your child feel loved, guess what? Nine times out of ten, that doesn't work with your spouse either. If you think that slaving all day cleaning the house and cooking dinner should make him or her feel loved, guess what? You are obviously missing each other like ships in the night. As I mentioned previously, Albert Einstein said that it's a sign of insanity to do the same things over and over and expect different results. Maybe it's time to change your tune.

> *Albert Einstein said that it's a sign of insanity to do the same things over and over and expect different results.*

Yes, it's awesome that you have a clean house, and that you cook healthy meals, but if you want your children to appreciate that, you have to meet their needs first. Your children need validation, your attention, and your interest in them—not just their compliance. It's amazing and commendable that you bring home money, but all kids need, more than anything else, is to know they are loved and that they are worth your time.

Of course, your children must learn obedience. Of course, your children must learn responsibility. Yes, they need to treat their siblings nicely and share their toys. Going to school and doing homework? Yes, you are right: they need to do that. But what good is being right if every day is a heart-wrenching battle for you and a wilderness of confusing emotions for them? What good is being right if you lose your kids to a group of equally confused young people who are more than willing to embrace and validate them?

You are right, Mom and Dad. You want your child to be a productive member of society. The best way to do that is to gain his or her cooperation. Stop pushing a wet noodle; it's time to jump in the water with your child and cook together.

TRY THIS FOR A WEEK:

- *Catch him doing the things you want him to do* and tell him you appreciate it—especially without being asked. "Wow, you are up and ready with time to spare this morning. How about if I make your favorite breakfast, since we have the time. I love having this extra, stress-free time with you."

- *Offer choices.* "Billy, is it more convenient for you to set the table before you do your homework or after?" "You can come in now if you want, or if you need more time, I'll call you in ten minutes." "Well, the cookies are for *after* dinner, but if you're hungry now, you could have some cheese and crackers or some yogurt or an apple. Which do you want?" Remember that your child might test you by pitching a fit. "I don't want an apple; I want a cookie!" Do not engage. Do not drop yourself to a seven-year-old level. Continue to act the adult and simply say, "Okay, well, just let me know if you change your mind."

- Provide lots of time for *outdoor and/or physical activities* to reduce stress.

- *Show him you notice and can anticipate his or her needs.* "Hey, I am going to throw a load in the washer; is there anything you need washed for school tomorrow?" If you show your child consideration, you teach him or her to do the same.

- *Create time to be together.* "Billy, I have to run to the store—want to come with me? We can stop and get ice cream on the way back." Or, "Let's plan a movie night this week. What's a good day for you, Billy?"

- *Make dinner conversation fun,* not a grilling session. Talk about funny things that happened that day. Talk about unusual news stories. "Did you hear that a new polar bear was born at the zoo? I heard they are having a contest to name her. Should we submit a suggestion?" If you and your spouse need to discuss heavy-duty financial matters, make an appointment to do it after dinner. If you need to address something difficult, set a time to talk about it with your child; don't use dinnertime, because it's the only time you're all together.

- *Be specific when giving praise.* Don't just say, "You're awesome." Tell your child what he or she did that was awesome. Did your child have a positive attitude? Did he or she use a particularly striking color in a painting? Did he or she jump on the trampoline a record number of times? It doesn't matter—just be specific. It's hard to repeat being awesome. It's measureable and repeatable to jump on the trampoline one hundred times or to treat a sister kindly.

And give lots of hugs when you can, snuggle when you can, and even roughhouse with him when you can. Kids need physical affection, and sometimes boys like to wrestle!

My Child Doesn't "Fit" into the School System

"Here's to the crazy ones. The misfits. The rebels. The trouble-makers. The round pegs in the square holes. The ones who see things differently. They're not fond of rules. And they have no respect for the status quo. You can quote them, disagree with them, glorify or vilify them. About the only thing you can't do is ignore them. Because they change things. They push the human race forward. And while some may see them as the crazy ones, we see genius. Because the people who are crazy enough to think they can change the world, are the ones who do."
—From the "Think Different" marketing campaign by Apple Inc.

If you worry that your kid doesn't run and play enough now that schools don't offer recess any more, or if you wonder if your kids will get a good education even though teachers admittedly have to teach to the standardized tests—allowing little room for individuality, focused attention, real creativity, and critical thinking—you are not alone.

So what does a parent do? You can complain to your neighbors; you can feel bitter and angry at the status quo; or you can jump right into your child's life and help him or her so he or she doesn't drown in the swirling sea of bureaucracy and political correctness.

Of course, we don't want our children to be outcasts. We want the teachers to like and respect our children. We want them to have good, trustworthy friends, and we want them to be safe. More than anything, we want them to feel good about themselves, to stand strong, and to get a good education so they can make valuable contributions to society and fully live the lives they were created to live.

A child's most important security comes from the home: from you. You can help him or her negotiate the scary waters of the real world by filling in the gaps at home. A child's character is largely formed by the time he or she is six, so you have six years to instill a strong sense of self, a determination that will keep him or her from giving up, and a secure environment that your child can return to at the end of the day to lick his or her wounds and fill his or her emotional bank account for the next day.

> A child's most important security comes from the home: from you.

There will always be times when your kid will not fit in, but this does not have to be a source of despair for you. You do not want a cookie-cutter kid. You do not want a child who has to hide who he really is to please some bureaucracy. But you can teach him how his uniqueness can enhance his environment. You can teach your child ways to get his needs met within the framework provided in the school system.

Life is full of expectations—no matter where your child goes. I know people who take their kids out of the public schools only to find that religious schools, private schools, or even homeschooling have their own challenges. Even as adults, we have to learn to "bloom where we are planted" and not die on the vine.

Many children, particularly boys, must express themselves kinesthetically, finding ways to release energy or anxiety by way of physical expression. All kids have this need to some extent—but some more than others. If this is the case with your children, make sure they get plenty of time every day to run outside and play at home. Perhaps go in and speak to the teachers about what outlets they provide in school for the kids to do this. Taking playtime away from a highly physical child is counterproductive. It's like putting a lid on a pressure cooker with no release valve and then punishing the pressure cooker for exploding. Be an advocate for your kids in the schools. Be vocal in the parent–teacher organization. Offer to help in some way at the school. This will benefit the situation in many ways. A teacher will be more amenable to help a child whose parent is not just a complainer but is someone who actually wants to help. Most teachers are overburdened and underfunded. How might you be an asset (keeping in mind that a "helicopter parent" is not an asset but a liability)? You should also limit your involvement: meaning that you have to trust the teacher to do what he or she is paid to do.

If your child seems to be slipping through the cracks academically, talk to the teacher about how you might help her at home. Spending pressure-free time at home reading with your younger children, having a reading time for the family, or even expecting everyone to read for a time each day sets a great example and encourages inquisitiveness and curiosity. Family research projects offer a fun way for kids to figure out how to discover things and how to obtain information. Parents who do not do everything for their kids—but rather encourage them to think things through and find answers on their own—help their children develop strong thinking patterns. In this way, you can help your child hone her skills at home in a friendly, loving atmosphere.

> Parents who do not do everything for their kids— but rather encourage them to think things through and find answers on their own— help their children develop strong thinking patterns.

Bullying is another problem we encounter more and more. No parent wants to see their child picked on by others. Sometimes, the schools are unaware of everything that is going on. So, if you suspect your child is being singled out for negative attention by her peers, bring the matter to the attention of the teacher and administrators so that they can be on the lookout and help provide a solution. Meanwhile, at home, you can teach her about the importance of empathy and personal responsibility. You can teach her about standing strong in her values and being kind to everyone. You can teach your child, as well, that there are reasons people act the way they do, and it doesn't have to affect her negatively. Just because a bully lashes out because he or she feels insecure and hurt doesn't mean there is anything wrong with your child. She can learn to discern when the problem is hers and when the problem is someone else's. She can identify how to put up boundaries and protect herself without internalizing the projections of the bully. These are all things you can help your child with at home.

I hear a lot of different fears of parents; these are but a few. In general, the most effective thing you can do as a parent is nurture a strong relationship with your child and encourage sharing and discussion without fear of judgment, ridicule, or, worse yet, indifference. When your child feels comfortable talking with you—sharing strong and sometimes scary emotions with you—and if he or she knows that you are discerning enough to know when he or she seems out of sorts, your child will likely feel free to share more information with you before it gets to be a huge problem.

The biggest danger is being too busy to create this kind of relationship or too overwhelmed ourselves to notice when something is going on with our child. We think we don't have time to talk to the teacher or volunteer at school. Keep in mind that if your kid gets in trouble or acts out and you get a call from the school or the police, you magically find the time to show up, but by then, you are angry and embarrassed. It's just like our physical health, where preventative checkups and healthy living keep much of the bad stuff at bay. A trusting relationship is your best preventative medicine.

The schools will never be able to do it all, and your children will have times when they don't feel like they fit in. Remind them daily—by way of your strong love and support—of their value just as they are and of the ways they can fit into the "framework" by staying true to who they are without becoming a clone of everyone else.

Again, let me reiterate that just telling them to be inquisitive and not being inquisitive yourself will not work. Telling them to put up healthy boundaries without having your own healthy boundaries will teach nothing. Encouraging them to release stress and frustration in healthy ways is great, but if that's not what you do, they won't do it either. Your example of a strong character is their best teacher. Yes, it takes diligence, but you are able to do it. Just keep practicing the secrets you've learned here.

HOW CAN I PROTECT MY CHILD
FROM SEXUAL ABUSE?

"Every now and then, we hear something on the news that is
so horrific we think it could never happen to our family.
We like to think we have complete control."
—*Mommy-Zen.com*

The news of the Sandusky sex abuse allegations caused many parents to question what they would do in such a situation. How would they even know? Such frightening scenarios often paralyze us or throw us into a frantic anxiety—neither of which is productive or helpful to our kids. The most important and powerful questions we can ask are: "What can we do about it?" and "How can we protect our kids?" Awareness and preparedness, not fear, are our best weapons against such a tragedy.

You must first realize that most molesters are not strangers to the children they victimize. Ninety percent of abusers are someone the child knows and trusts. Also, the abuse will most likely not start with sexual activity. Most of the Sandusky victims admit that it started with special treatment: gifts, benefits, and a growing relationship. Abusers often use these things to break down the child's resistance and instincts.

Charlyn Hasson-Brown, Chief Executive Director of CASA (Court Appointed Special Advocates of Prince William and Fauquier, www.casaofgpw.org), says that predators can be charming, manipulative, and deceitful. She encourages parents to keep their children from being alone with anyone that they are not 100 percent sure can be trusted. This includes: relatives, teachers, coaches, neighbors, and lovers.

So, parents ask, "What are the main warning signs that your child may have been sexually abused?" Hasson-Brown offers these indicators from Prevent Child Abuse America. Consider it a red flag if your child:

1. Has trouble walking or sitting;

2. Displays knowledge of or interest in sexual acts inappropriate to his or her age or displays seductive behavior;

3. Makes strong efforts to avoid a certain person without an obvious reason;

4. Doesn't want to change clothes in front of others or participate in physical activities;

5. Has an STD or pregnancy under the age of fourteen; or

6. Runs away from home.

Some other warning signs to look for in young children (from www.hhs.gov) include:

1. Compulsive, frequent masturbation,

2. Sex play with toys,

3. Drawing pictures of sexual activity,

4. Sleep disturbances, or

5. Cruelty to animals.

For older kids, watch for:

1. Eating disturbances,

2. Criminal activity,

3. Self-destructive behavior, or

4. Depression and withdrawal

While most of these are not certain indicators, they give you a place to begin the discussion—which needs to happen. Your kids need a safe place to talk. So, how can you make that happen?

First, you must *believe* your child if she tells you that someone has touched her inappropriately. It's difficult to do, particularly if the perpetrator is someone you trust, someone high profile, or someone with a great reputation (like Sandusky).

The facts report that only one to five percent of accusations are fabricated, so the odds are good that your child is telling you the truth. React with compassion: not anger, panic, or disgust—which will shut your kids down, thinking they told you something inappropriate that you cannot handle. They might even think that you feel disgusted or angry with *them*. Stay calm, ask open-ended questions, and validate their feelings. "That must have been very confusing and scary for you." Continue to reassure them that they are very brave, and that they did the right thing by telling you, and that you have the ability to handle the situation.

It's also important to trust your instincts. If you notice changes in your child, gently address the subject. Tell your child that you've noticed that she doesn't seem to be herself lately, and that you are available to talk. Young children are very suggestible, so you don't want to suggest that a certain person did a certain thing. This is a good time to take a few minutes to talk to her about inappropriate touching, even if your child says nothing has happened. During this talk, you should use proper names to label body parts. Kids should never feel like there is anything embarrassing about—or wrong with—their bodies. Explain the difference between good touches and bad touches. Start by explaining that a bathing suit covers the private parts of their bodies, and that no one should be able to touch them in those places. You can specify exceptions: like a trusted parent, doctor, or other specified person for a specified reason, such as bathing, check-ups, etc. Your kids should tell you about any touch that makes them uncomfortable.

If they are afraid to tell you, they can tell a trusted teacher or counselor.

You should also stress to your kids that your family keeps no secrets—ever. You might keep surprises (like a birthday gift or surprise party)—but no secrets. Make sure your kids understand that it's always okay to tell you anything; you will not overreact. Even if someone threatens to hurt them if they tell, you can handle it. You need to assure them of this.

There are several good resources to help you have this conversation with a young child. One of them is a book called *My Body Belongs to Me* by Jill Starishevsky. It offers a straightforward approach to helping a child recognize acceptable and unacceptable behaviors and when and to whom they can talk about it.

If your child reveals that something has happened, it's important for you as a parent to follow through and ask for help so you can all get the support you need. Call Child Protective Services (CPS) to report what you know. If there are legal issues to pursue, they can help walk you through them. Then, call a therapist to help you and your child work through the fear and shame as well.

Even as I was writing this chapter, I received a call from a person with an inquiry about what you do if you suspect sexual abuse involving someone else's child. If your child witnesses something, even at a neighbor's house, you should act on it—but not overreact. Tell the parents of the other child. Call CPS and file a report or ask questions. You should only allow your

Here are some resources to help you get your questions answered:
www.stopitnow.org
www.darkness2light.org
Child Protective Services
Child Abuse Hotline: 1-800-552-7096

child to play with another child under close supervision if that child displays questionable behaviors.

Most importantly, stay informed, prepare your kids, and protect them as best you can: not by instilling fear but by instilling wisdom.

1. Use any opportunity to bring the topic up.

    a. I was just thinking....
    b. I just read an article....
    c. I just heard a story on the news....
    d. I want to talk about something important with you....

2. You may feel uncomfortable talking about this or think you may scare your children. The truth is you probably feel more uncomfortable than they will. You talk to them about escape routes in case of a fire, safe meeting places in case they get lost at the mall, or how to behave in an earthquake. Your kids don't freak out about that; neither should you. This is similar: a strategy of preparation. Hopefully, none of these things ever happen; it's just good to be prepared.

3. Use the proper terms for body parts. Your children should never be taught to be ashamed of their bodies.

4. Discuss what constitutes a good touch and a bad touch.

5. Talk about not having secrets.

6. Tell your children that their *"No!"* should be respected in cases like this (if they say no to tickling or hugging or kissing). Don't *force* them to kiss or hug anyone or consent to being tickled. Just teach your kids to be polite.

7. Tell them that if they feel uncomfortable and someone tries to touch them inappropriately, they should yell and run.

8. If someone threatens your children or someone they love, stress that they should still tell you because bullies' barks are worse than their bites, and you are not afraid.

9. Create an open home environment where everyone is believed and respected in your family—no matter how young they are.

10. Practice being calm and not overreacting to anything; this way, your kids will feel safe talking to you.

11. Be aware of your children's activities and behaviors so you will recognize if something is out of whack.

12. Educate yourself to normal behaviors at various stages of development.

13. Be aware of any adult or older child who wants to spend an unusual amount of time with your child alone.

14. Spend time with your kids. Encourage discussions.

15. If your children ever feel unsafe talking to you (which happens sometimes, especially with teens), give some suggestions of trusted adults: like a pastor, teacher, or counselor.

FEELING GUILTY AFTER YOUR OWN MELTDOWN?

"Fall down seven times; get up eight" —Japanese Proverb
"Though a righteous man falls seven times, he rises again"
—Proverbs 24:17

Her kids were screaming, crying, and complaining. Nothing seemed to be going right. This single mom explained how she kept her composure as long as she could, until she finally stopped the car and let out an eardrum-shattering scream. It shut the kids up, all right. She screamed that she was finished with all this crap, and her kids had better straighten up or else!

Silence.

Even though a meltdown can have an immediate effect and can stun kids into compliance, it's not the healthiest way to communicate your feelings. The truth is we have all had these moments when we see no other option than to scream, yell, or even hit. These episodes are almost always immediately followed by incredible, heavy remorse. So what do you do?

Sometimes, moms will hope the kids forget about it and not mention it. Sometimes, they will feel so guilty that they give the kids whatever they want. But neither of these responses is optimal.

The first thing to do is to acknowledge to your kids what just happened. Start by apologizing for the outburst. "Wow, I just had a real meltdown, didn't I? I am so sorry." Then use the opportunity, while you have everyone's attention, to create a teaching moment. Do not get caught up in self-defense. The kids did *not* make you respond that way. The devil did not make you respond that way. This is your chance to humbly and honestly show your kids that a healthy person always accepts responsibility for his or her actions.

"Please understand that is never the best way to handle a situation. We always have choices." And then take it step-by-step with your kids to find a new solution. "Let's rewind for a few minutes and do this right. I felt really angry and frustrated because you were not getting dressed quickly enough for school, and now we are late. Next time, I will have to get up earlier (or make lunches the night before, or choose outfits the night before, or whatever will remedy the problem). Please forgive me."

Here are some pointers to help you remember:

1. Acknowledge the meltdown.

2. Apologize.

3. Accept total responsibility for your response (no blaming, no defensiveness).

4. Use the opportunity to make it a teaching moment.

5. Rewind and start over.

6. Acknowledge and name your feelings.

7. State the reason for the emotions, without blaming.

8. Offer what you can do differently next time.

9. Ask for forgiveness. This is not the same as apologizing. An apology is a statement of regret. As important as that is, apologizing differs from asking for forgiveness. When you ask your children to forgive you, you empower them to choose to clear the air. They learn that they can choose to let something go. They learn that people (even Mommy) can make mistakes and be forgiven—which means they can too!

10. Affirm your love for them, perhaps with a hug.

After you take care of *your* part, ask your kids for suggestions on how they might help. "Do you have a thought on how *you* might be able to help make things go smoother in the mornings?"

Of course, with all the talk about forgiveness, you must absolutely admit to yourself that you are human and have your "moments." Forgiving yourself is crucial because it will set the example for your kids to know that they should do the same. We all need to leave the past in the past. The more you drag around with you in the form of guilt, anger, hurt, regret, and unforgiveness, the more difficult you will find effective parenting. You will spend so much time focusing on the past that you will lose sight of the future, and the present moment (which is really all you have) will slip right through your fingers.

THE COMMITMENT: A MILLION
MINDFUL MOMS

"I have a dream...." —*Martin Luther King, Jr.*
"Be the change you want to see in the world."
—*Mahatma Gandhi*

I have asked myself what the world would look like if we really took our job as parents seriously. I know you do, or you wouldn't be reading this book—and you certainly wouldn't be near the end!

Do we realize that we are actually raising tomorrow's leaders? I think we often discount our kids and their potential. Sure, we tell them they can be anything they want to be; they can do anything they put their minds to. But do we really believe that?

Dr. Ben Carson is a world-famous pediatric neurosurgeon who, in 1987, became the first surgeon ever to successfully separate conjoined twins connected at the back of the head. A movie called *Gifted Hands* tells his story.

Dr. Carson, of course, wasn't always a world-famous doctor. He was a poor student with a hot temper, raised by a depressed single mother who couldn't read. But his mom did not let her limitations and his shortcomings cloud her vision of what he could be. She encouraged him to read; she cut his television time; she required written book reports; she overcame her own depression; and she learned to read. She set an example for her kids of overcoming the odds and persevering, never losing her faith, and knowing that God had great things for her kids to do.

Your kids are no different from Dr. Ben Carson. Your limitations are no more overwhelming than his mom's. But she had vision. She felt a kind of obligation to make the most of herself and to help her kids do the same. Her son, because of her focus and clear vision, has clearly changed the world. Other moms have raised kids who have overcome the odds as well.

Don't forget Hannah, who was willing to keep her promise to God—knowing him to be faithful—so that Samuel became a great prophet; he changed his world, all because his mom trusted God and believed that he had great things in store for her son. There are many such stories in the Bible—Moses, Isaac, Jesus, and more—stories of children who overcame great odds and parents with steadfast focus and faith who raised them so that they changed the world.

We each have unlimited potential. We need to develop that and teach our kids to develop their unique gifts as well. But we fritter away the time. We think nothing's really happening because we don't see immediate results; and we get bored or lose focus, and our faith falters.

I have a vision. You are in that vision. I believe that there are a million mindful moms (dads, grandparents, aunts, and uncles included!) all over the world, willing to commit to practicing the principles of peaceful parenting, to take the time and effort, and to fully expect to change the world.

WHO IS A MINDFUL MOM?

She is willing to commit to following The 10 Essential Principles of Peaceful Parenting. She is willing to:

- Connect regularly to her creator,

- Know and live out her true identity,

- Nurture her awareness,

- Breathe before she speaks or acts,

- Respect herself and others,

- Practice gratitude regularly,

- Limit judgments,

- Detach when necessary,

- Communicate effectively, and

- Forgive quickly.

It's not so hard; it just takes commitment. Even if you struggle to practice these regularly, you can change just one action at a time, one day at a time, and one week at a time. Choose one principle to put into practice and concentrate on that one thing for a week; then, add the second and the third and so on until you have incorporated all the regular practices. Presto! In ten weeks, you will be on your way to living the mindful life, remembering that it is not a destination; it is a journey—a lifestyle.

With the quiet power and peaceful demeanor you will exude, other parents will catch on and want to be like you. You can join MommyZen's online group and support each other. For admission, you need only to tell me that you have bought or acquired the book and have committed to practicing the 10 Principles for Peaceful Parenting. You will benefit, your kids will benefit, and together, we will change the world!

For those of you who are *really serious* and need a *change quickly,*
order this *life changing* program

From Chaos to Calm in 30 Days!

For more information go to mommy-zen.com.

THE HAND THAT ROCKS THE CRADLE IS THE HAND THAT RULES THE WORLD

by William Ross Wallace

BLESSINGS on the hand of women!
Angels guard its strength and grace.
In the palace, cottage, hovel,
Oh, no matter where the place;
Would that never storms assailed it,
Rainbows ever gently curled,
For the hand that rocks the cradle
Is the hand that rules the world.
Infancy's the tender fountain,
Power may with beauty flow,
Mothers first to guide the streamlets,
From them souls unresting grow—
Grow on for the good or evil,
Sunshine streamed or evil hurled,

For the hand that rocks the cradle
Is the hand that rules the world.
Woman, how divine your mission,
Here upon our natal sod;
Keep—oh, keep the young heart open
Always to the breath of God!
All true trophies of the ages
Are from mother-love impearled,
For the hand that rocks the cradle
Is the hand that rules the world.
Blessings on the hand of women!
Fathers, sons, and daughters cry,
And the sacred song is mingled
With the worship in the sky—
Mingles where no tempest darkens,
Rainbows evermore are hurled;
For the hand that rocks the cradle
Is the hand that rules the world.

A FINAL WORD
IS IT TOO LATE?

"It's never too late—in fiction or in life—to revise."
—Nancy Thayer

A fair amount of parents confide in me their concern that they are screwing up their kids. As a matter of fact, I think it is a secret fear of most parents from time to time.

Like many of my readers, I also have grown children. Knowing that I did not do everything right or well, I basically have to continue to love them the best I can, be there for support when they need me, and pay for their therapy if they need it!

My very first mentor, Georgianna Rodiger, of the Georgianna Rodiger Center in Pasadena, California, shared the following bits of wisdom with me. First, she said, "Marianne, if you are afraid...you will never be a good therapist." Having five grown kids of her own, she added, "I did the best I knew how at the time, and, if necessary, I will pay for their therapy." Her fearlessly loving approach to therapy and her thoughts about moving forward and doing the best you can have provided real inspiration for me to be not only a fearless mom but also a fearless therapist.

Understanding that everyone has meltdowns from time to time, and that everyone overreacts sometimes, and that everyone has a bad day once in a while, it's important to learn to leave yesterday behind and move on. You cannot fix actions already taken, but you have free reign to embrace each opportunity you have today to act in a good, kind, and loving way.

The Bible says, "What I feared has come upon me; what I dreaded has happened to me. I have no peace, no quietness; I have no rest, but only turmoil." (Job 3:25–26) We can create self-fulfilling prophecies in our lives if we put all our energy into what we dread might happen or what we fear or regret. There is no better time to start doing the right thing than today. Practice the ten essential principles of peaceful parenting, knowing that they apply to both parents and non-parents alike. It's never too late.

Here is a verse that I have embraced over the years when I felt my kids straying from the path that I thought was best for them; it has given me much comfort. Not only that, but I have seen our kids grow into healthy, productive adults (many with wonderful families of their own)—a huge source of joy for me!

"Thus saith the LORD: 'Restrain thy voice from weeping, and thine eyes from tears; for thy work shall be rewarded,' saith the LORD; 'and they shall come back from the land of the enemy. And there is hope in thine end,' saith the LORD, 'that thy children shall come back to their own border.'" Jeremiah 31:1–17

About the Author

Marianne Clyde is a licensed marriage and family therapist, author, coach and speaker. She helps people break through those barriers that keep them from living the abundant life they were created to live.

She has practiced as a therapist in California, Massachusetts, Virginia, and Tokyo, Japan. In developing her skills as an international expert on empowerment, she has been privileged to travel to over forty countries—about half of those being developing countries—where she has taught healing from trauma, personal growth, and empowerment.

A mom and stepmom to eight grown kids and a grandma to ten grandchildren, she currently lives in Virginia in the foothills of the Blue Ridge Mountains with her husband Bob and their two labs, Mojo and Pepper.

Made in the USA
Charleston, SC
10 July 2013